Fit to Be Tied

Fit to Be Tied

Ontario's Murderous Past

Terry Boyle

Polar Bear Press, Toronto

Polar
Bear
Press

Distributed by
North 49 Books
35 Prince Andrew Place
Toronto, Ontario
M3C 2H2
(416) 449-4000

National Library of Canada Canadian Cataloguing in Publication Data

Boyle Terry, 1953-
   Fit to be tied: Ontario's murderous past

Includes biographical references and index
ISBN 1-896757-15-4

1. Murder — Ontario — History. 2. Hanging — Ontario — History. I. Title
HV6535.C32065 2001a   364.15′23′09713   C2001-930676-8

2001 02 03 04 10 9 8 7 6 5 4 3 2 1
Printed in Canada

Front cover image: National Archives of Canada

Book designed by Fortunato Design Inc.

Table of Contents

NOTES ON THE HANGMEN

British executioner William Marwood stated "Most executioners had to depend on other trades to supplement their income because money they made on executions was small and they happened on an infrequent basis." In Canada executioners were sometimes condemned prisoners. When executions were public events, the executioners became public celebrities, although it was usually advisable for them to keep their identity private. Public executions could be just as dangerous for the executioner as it was for the condemned. If the condemned suffered on the scaffolding, the crowd could riot and lynch the hangman. As a general rule, executioners, despite their public status, were shunned by most people. A lot of them lived solitary lives and became alcoholics. It was not uncommon for a hangman to get drunk prior to a hanging or to do so afterward.

Jack Ketch was one of the earliest hangmen in Britain. In fact, after his death his name became the alias for all executioners. However, Jack was inept at his job of hanging and beheading and he frequently bungled. He was also in trouble with the law because of his debts. Eventually he was replaced but was rehired when the new man had to be hung for murder.

William Marwood thought hanging was a science. He tried to make it less painful for the condemned by breaking the neck instead of strangulation. He did this by strengthening the straps and adding a metal ring to the noose. This metal ring would serve as the signature of all future British hangings.

Arthur Ellis was the pseudonym for Arthur Bartholomew English. He was Canada's most famous hangman and travelled across the country to hang the condemned. He supplemented his pay by working at a Toronto yacht club under his proper name. When an RCMP officer recognized him and complained to the management, the club fired him. His other career came to an end in 1935 when he decapitated Thomasino Sarao. Ellis had calculated the drop for a 145 lb. woman when, in fact, Sarao weighted 187 lbs. Prison officials had given him the incorrect weight. Ellis died in 1938. Today a prestigious crime writers' award is named for him.

Introduction

*A*s a special education teacher in Care, Custody and Treatment settings in the province of Ontario, my job has always involved troubled youth and I have worked with them in psychiatric hospitals, group homes and jails. My secondment from the Durham District School Board at Project Turnaround, the first book camp for repeat offenders, was an education in itself.

The mental, emotional and physical difficulties young people are experiencing in our society today are major issues that frequently lead to lives of crime.

Crime is an act of unconscious thought, often rooted in childhood. The criminal actions of a person are seldom consciously associated with any specific memory. The individual is simply no longer able to function in society with any kind of balance.

People speak of the bad crime rate these days; some even speak about the return of capital punishment. Many Canadians feel the cost is too high for housing and rehabilitating criminals. And then there are those who quote the Old Testament, "An eye for an eye..."

A common theme today is "the system no longer works". We certainly hear about and see those who have been victimized. It is, nevertheless, a rarity to hear anyone compare the crimes of today to the crimes of the past. That is one reason I decided to write this book. The crimes of the past are just as heinous as those committed today. The criminals are just as dastardly.

Another motivating factor for me was the fate of our historic jails. The sale of government real estate, particularly our heritage buildings, including jails, demands that some record be made while the information is still available.

It was shocking for me to realize the fascination people have for crime. The criminal trials that resulted in hangings were a form of entertainment. Today the media provides the same source of entertainment through grotesque accounts of heinous crimes. Our ancestors got their entertainment from real-life drama and would travel miles to witness a hanging.

Rape, abortion, theft and murder were common occurrences throughout the 19th and 20th centuries in Ontario. The law of the land was often swift and deadly but was it thorough and was it just? Were the guilty always hanged and were the hanged always guilty?

I hope this book provokes, amazes and fascinates you, even as it did me during the research and writing.

TERRY BOYLE
Parry Sound, Ontario

The Melbourne Home Bank Robbery

At midnight on February 10, 1924, Sidney Murrell of London, Ontario sat up on his jail cell bed and greeted his spiritual advisor, Reverend Quintin Warner of the Anglican Church. Together with cell mate Clarence Topping, Sidney spent the last night of his life singing hymns, praying and confessing. He spoke calmly and at length about his mother, his family and the friends who still cared about him.

SIDNEY MURRELL

Topping had been besotted with love for a Miss Durston. She, on the other hand, had refused to marry him. Early one morning, in an aggravated state, he came to her apartment. She phoned for the police. Topping forced his way into the bedroom where Miss Durston and her friend, Miss Viola McNaughton, had taken refuge. He threatened to kill her unless she promised to marry him. George Cook, the owner and landlord of the house demanded that Topping leave and then went himself to fetch the local constable. Before the officer could reach the bedroom, two shots rang out in quick succession, followed by a third retort. Two bullets pierced Miss Durston's abdomen and one bullet struck Miss McNaughton in the chest. Miss Durston died on the way to the hospital; her friend recovered from her wounds.

Convicted of the murder, he now waited for death with his cell mate, Sidney Murrell.

Each of the condemned men were served a three o'clock breakfast that consisted of toast and coffee, and then Mr. Warner left. Sheriff Graham, attired in the garb of his office, a dress suit and a silk hat, arrived at the London jail at 5:17 a.m. Representatives of the press and others were already gathered. As the execution hour approached, so did Arthur Ellis. He was the hangman, attired in a black morning suit as he came forward from the office of the governor in the jail. In each hand he carried a tumbler half full of whiskey mixed with liquid morphine, which was given to the prisoners as a tranquilizer. Newspaper men and visitors were then ushered into the corridor below where instructions of procedure were quickly given by the executioner before the visitors were ushered out to the gallows.

According to *The London Free Press*, "Sheriff Donald Graham, Jail Governor Byron Dawson and several guards entered the common cell where both prisoners awaited the hangman."

Murrell inquired, "Are the newspaper representatives here?"

He was denied their audience and so he made his statement short. "My time has come to part with this world. Good luck and God bless you."

He thanked his keepers for the kind treatment shown him since his incarceration there; he thanked the friends who had shown an interest in him and expressed regret that he could not take with him the grief he was to leave behind.

Murrell told officials that he would make no attempt to fight the hangman when the time came to adjust the straps, and he kept his word. Topping followed Murrell's example: at 5:31 a.m. the short march to the scaffold began. Both Murrell and Topping smiled as they passed the small group of men who were to witness the execution.

Hangman Ellis was a small man of about 50 years who walked with a short, quick step. He wore gold rimmed glasses, and seemed unconcerned with his onerous duty. One newspaper account described Ellis as a man who carried out executions with a quickness and dispatch scarcely to be believed. His demeanour was quiet and unassuming, not at all the stereotypical executioner.

Murrell and Topping chose to wear their own clothes in lieu of prison garb; aside from smiles for the press, they both looked straight ahead. The London paper added, "There was no faltering as the scaffold was reached. Those who witnessed the execution were astonished at the celerity (swiftness) shown by the hangman."

Scuffling feet could be heard as the hangman put black caps over the heads of the condemned men and adjusted the nooses. They stood side by side on the narrow platform. Seconds later they fell and at the end there was an audible, low moan.

Hangman Ellis proceeded so quickly that Reverend Quinton Warner had no opportunity to repeat the Lord's Prayer, which customarily marked the end. The jail physician, Dr. J.D. Wilson, said that death was instantaneous.

On that same fateful morning Mrs. Murrell stood before a window in a tiny home on Clarence Street in London. She raised the blind to let the soft, warm rays of sun find their way into a house filled with sorrow. Only minutes before, her son had paid for his wrongdoing with his life. As strange as it may seem, his father had left only moments later for work, lunch pail in hand.

Concealed Weapons at Public Meetings: It is wrong to carry concealed weapons in Canada and you must not come armed within two miles of a public meeting without incurring a penalty of $100 upon conviction. If you molest any person returning from a public meeting designedly, either by personal violence or by using opprobrious epithets, you can be fined $200 or go to jail for six months.

An eerie feeling lingered at the hanging site. White frost covered the gallows and the prisoners' footprints were still visible. In that moment doubts surfaced — did they hang the wrong man?

Sidney Murrell was born in England on November 2, 1899. He immigrated to Canada and settled in London, Ontario with his parents in April of 1906. Sydney and his elder brother William were athletic young men, both skilled in wrestling and boxing. To his intimate friends Syd was known as 'Curly'.

At the outbreak of World War I, Sydney lied about his age and was subsequently stationed overseas for the duration of the war. It was rumoured that he had a family there who stayed behind on his return home.

After the war, Sidney drifted from one job to another. He and William were often up to no good. They terrorized a Chinese launderer once, robbed him and cut off his sacred pony tail.

However, many evenings were still spent in the Murrell family home with Sidney playing the piano convivially while friends gathered around to sing popular tunes. In 1921 two new faces, Henry (Slim) Williams and Pat Norton joined the Murrell brothers' social circle. Evenings were now spent discussing plans for the future. Pat Norton, who was in his thirties and much older than the others, may have introduced the subject of bank robberies to the Murrell brothers. After all, they did need money and banks seemed to have just that! They agreed to set out from London on foot to stage a bank hold-up in Windsor. One of them knew where to steal a car at Byron, just five miles from London.

At 6 a.m. on April 11, 1921, four strangers in a stolen automobile travelled slowly down the main street of Melbourne, Ontario. The occupants of the car were Sidney, his brother William, Henry (Slim) Williams and Pat Norton. As they passed a hotel Pat asked Sidney to pull over so he could go in and get some cigarettes. William joined him. Once back in the car Sidney started down the road going about 30 miles an hour as they passed the Home Bank. Someone in the car said that would be a good bank to rob. At the next crossroads, Sydney turned north and then west again and turned into a bush on property owned by George J. Stevenson. There they built a small fire and slept for a couple of hours before turning their attention back to Melbourne. Sitting around the fire William, Henry and Sidney pulled out their guns. William and Slim owned .38 caliber revolvers and Sidney owned a 45. Pat did not participate in the show and tell.

The boys talked about going back to Melbourne and robbing the Home Bank. They discussed a plan. It was simple. William was to go into the bank because he looked like a business man. He was wearing glasses, a bowler hat and a new overcoat. He looked the most respectable. Slim was to stay at the door and keep watch. Pat and Sidney would get the cash. The car would be parked out front and left running for a speedy getaway.

Shortly after eleven o'clock that morning their car came to a stop in front of the bank. William was the first to walk into the Home Bank followed by Pat, Sydney and Slim. Pat asked Sydney for his gun and Sydney complied.

Sydney was about ten feet from the bank manager's office when he heard someone yell out 'hands up' to R.E. McCandless, manager of the bank. He refused. Blows on the head, between the eyes and on the side of the face were answers to his refusal.

Bank employee Miss Campbell was seen down at the safe facing the east wall and apparently fastening the combination. Sydney rushed around to the teller's cage and opened the door. There was nothing in it. A drawer there, however, held bills of several denominations. Sydney held a bag to the drawer and started to scoop the bills. Meanwhile Miss Campbell rushed past Slim who, instead of guarding the front door, had stepped inside the bank. Campbell managed to reach the street and proceeded to give the alarm.

When Pat realized what had just happened he ordered Slim to get back to the door or he would drill him.

Slim returned only to yell, "Here they come".

William asked, "Who's coming?"

"A whole gang," answered Slim.

A group of villagers led by the Campbell brothers and manager E.T. Theaker of the Union Bank bore down on the bank.

Robert and Stuart Campbell entered the front door, while Russell walked down the lane beside the building.

Suddenly Sydney heard shots. He had no idea where they came from. Slim and William rushed into the manager's office. Sydney fled to the rear of the bank where he saw McCandless lying on the floor with his knees doubled under him as if his head was lying inside the safe. He might have been dead for all he knew. Stepping over the manager's body Sydney spotted a .45 caliber gun lying on the floor. He picked it up. By now Stuart Campbell and George Sponenburgh were facing Sydney. Stuart had a rifle and George a revolver.

Campbell yelled out, "Hands up. Hands up."

Sydney fired toward the ceiling and moved closer to the counter. Stuart Campbell was now on the other side bobbing up and down. His rifle was aimed directly at Sydney.

By now Robert Campbell was approaching. Sydney fired another shot through the window in the upper part of the door to attract his attention and stop him from proceeding. Robert kept on coming and Sydney no longer knew where Stuart Campbell was. Another shot was fired by Sydney in the direction of the east wall. It was total chaos. Sydney saw Slim rush out the side door that led to the alleyway and followed in close pursuit.

Before Sydney reached the main street he caught sight of Russell Campbell lying on the ground. His chest was to the ground and blood was running out of his nose. It looked to Sydney like Russell had been hit in the face with a brick.

Robert Campbell followed closely on his heels and grappled with Sydney who quickly threw Robert to the ground. Stuart Campbell who was just behind Robert grabbed Sydney by the coat tail while another citizen tripped him. The crowd on the street quickly assisted in apprehending Sydney.

In the meantime Slim was engaged in a revolver duet with E.T. Theaker, manager of the Union Bank. Slim was shot in the hand. Before Slim could fire again, the crowd grabbed him and lashed him and Sydney to a telephone pole in front of the Melbourne Hotel.

Meanwhile, William was hiding out in the hayloft of a barn located at the rear of the bank.

Wilfrid Denford, an Onieda Native from the Muncey Reserve, rushed into the barn after William and quickly climbed up into the hayloft. Even though William had a gun, Denford still pounced and apprehended him.

William refused to climb down so Wilfrid threw him out of the loft door to the street below where a group of villagers overpowered him and tied him to a post.

The citizens of Melbourne wasted no time pitching in to capture the bank robbers. They were zealous in overpowering the robbers and had no concern for their personal safety.

A man named Miles yelled out that his Ford car had just been stolen by the fourth bank robber. A group of armed men piled into a car and took chase down the sixteenth sideroad. Before they could catch him their car broke down. Pat continued on until he, too, experienced engine problems. Abandoning his car he fled on foot into the woods and was never seen again.

It wasn't long before the town folk were notified that Russell Campbell was dead from a gun-shot wound just below his heart. The mood of the residents of Melbourne quickly turned ugly. The cry was, "Lynch them!" One of the prisoners exclaimed, "Ladies and gentlemen", and then broke into sobs.

The police arrived and Detectives Nickle and Down from London transported the prisoners to the London Middlesex Jail.

Magistrate A.H.M. Graydon first laid a charge of robbing a Chinese laundry on the previous Saturday night. The prisoners pleaded guilty to this charge. The coroner's jury, which held an inquest for Russell Campbell on April 14, brought in a finding of 'murder by the three bandits'.

Sydney, William and Slim were placed in the same cell. During that summer Slim complained of mistreatment by the Murrell brothers. On one occasion in the yard William threw a toad at Slim. Governor

> 1921, Kingston: Norman Garfield was hung for the shooting of Ben Johnson during a hold-up in a confectionery story. Garfield vowed he would never hang and swallowed a quantity of ground glass. Doctors worked furiously to save his life and did so; he walked up the fateful 13 steps and was hanged.

Williams of the jail commented on the use of filthy language. He considered Slim to be a model prisoner. Slim was eventually removed and placed in a separate cell.

The Murrells' cell was the first locker at the foot of the stairs somewhat separated from the rest of the jail. Their beds were in one room and a lavatory was in another. In the lavatory was a window 2 feet by 3 feet.

On the night of September 2, 1921, Ellison Hodgins came on turnkey duty at 6 o'clock. At approximately 6:30 p.m. Hodgins turned on the lights and one of the Murrell brothers thanked him.

—$3,000 REWARDS—

Wanted For Murder and Robbery

Geo. Ernest 'Pat' Norton

Norton is wanted in London, Ontario on a charge of robbery with violence, bank hold-up and murder at Melbourne, Ontario, in April, 1921.

One thousand dollars reward is offered by The London Advertiser for his capture and arrest before Jan. 1, 1924.

DESCRIPTION

Age—35 or 37 years.
Height—5 feet, 8 or 9 inches.
Weight—160 pounds.
Eyes—Hazel.
Complexion—Rather light, sandy; may have mustache.
Occupation—Railroad man, lineman, automobile mechanic, waiter or teamster.

William Murrell

Murrell is wanted in London, Ontario, on a charge of robbery with violence, bank hold-up and murder at Melbourne, Ontario, in April, 1921.

Murrell escaped from London jail Sept. 2, 1921, and the Province of Ontario has offered two thousand dollars reward for information leading to his arrest.

DESCRIPTION

Age—25 years.
Height—5 feet 8 inches.
Weight—150 pounds.
Eyes—Hazel.
Complexion—Dark, with dark brown hair.
Marks—Star, snake, leg and bird tattooed on left arm; scar on back of right hand.

Persons having information regarding these men are asked to communicate with

ROBERT BIRRELL, Chief Constable, London, Ont.

or DONALD A. GRAHAM, Sheriff, County of Middlesex, Ontario

or THE LONDON ADVERTISER, London, Ontario

At 6:45 p.m. the Turnkey heard the Murrell brothers singing. Ellison returned at 8 p.m. to lock them in for the night only to discover they were gone and a small saw lay on the floor. The brothers had cunningly escaped by cutting the bars of their jail cell window.

A few weeks before a wall had been built to divide the yard in two and a shed for county road machinery was being built on one side. Two ladders had been left in the yard even though the workers had been warned not to leave anything on the premises. It seems that the Murrells used one of these ladders against the southeast wall, to assist in their escape.

Provincial authorities immediately offered rewards for their capture, in total, $4,000. A description of the prisoners appeared in numerous papers. It read: "William G. Murrell, aged 25, height 5 feet 7 inches, weight 150 pounds, complexion dark, hair dark brown eyes hazel, snake and bird tattooed on left arm, scar on back of right hand. Sidney E. Murrell, aged 22, height 5 feet 8 inches, weight 155 pounds, complexion fresh, hair brown, eyes hazel, American eagle tattooed on chest, Buffalo Bill, American flag; St. George with Cross, sunflower tattooed on left arm, Scotch soldier and boxing boy tattooed on right arm, and three scars on forehead." Not average-looking boys.

Police and jail officials began an investigation concerning the saw that was used in the escape. They wanted to know who delivered the saw to the cell.

Their mother was a prime suspect.

On September 6th, *The Toronto Star* published this account of an interview with Mrs. Mabel Jane Murrell, mother of Sydney and William, while she was visiting Mrs. Edmundson, a friend of Sydney's in Toronto.

"With Mrs. Murrell is Mrs. Ada Edmundson, a friend of Sydney Murrell. The mother says that she last saw her boys in the London jail a week ago last Saturday, while Mrs. Edmundson declares that the last time she saw or spoke with the prisoners was on August 19, also in the jail at London.

"Mrs. Murrell says: 'I know nothing about the escape. The first time I knew that they had got away was on Saturday morning, when

I read it in the paper.'

"'Have you heard from them since?'

"No, not a line.'

"'Were you ever in their cell?'

"'No, when I called to see them I had to stand outside the cell door and speak to them through a hole in the door. All the stuff I brought them I handed to the turnkey.'

"'Why did you come to Toronto?'

"'I came here to visit Mrs. Edmundson, but I am going back to London. I have nothing to fear. The police there know where I am. The Toronto police have interviewed me.'

"'Did you think your boys should have tried to get away?'

"'No, the last time I spoke to them I told them to face the music.'"

To the reporter Mrs Edmundson explained her friendship with Sidney Murrell and the Murrell family.

"'I met Sydney Murrell when he was a boy of 16, overseas in the Moore Barracks Hospital at Folkestone. He was injured and I wrote to his mother - after that I never saw him again till I spoke to him in the cells at London.'

"'How did you come to meet them again?'

"'I lost track of them until they were arrested after the holdup at Melbourne, when I read the account in the paper. Then I wrote to Mrs. Murrell and was invited to London.'

"'Was Sydney the cause of separating you from your husband?'

"'Sydney had nothing to do with it, and you can see my husband. He is living on Manning Avenue. I have not seen Sydney since I left London on August 19.'

"'But the London police claim you were in London the day the boys escaped.'

"'That is not so, and I know nothing of the affair.'

Police officials were stumped. No suspect was ever charged in assisting the Murrell brothers to escape.

At the same time a letter purporting to be written by one of the Murrells at the time of the jail break arrived by mail at the office of *The Free Press* newspaper. Here it is, errors included:

"Dear Sir: Just a few lines to the Press. As no doubt you will all be looking for some news after our wonderful escape. Well, we found it quite a joy to have the pleasure of the good air that we have mist for quite a long time. But while I am dooping you these few lines I must say that the Lon-

The formidable London jail could not contain the mischievous Murrell brothers.

don police are very slow, as it was only 30 minutes after we was out we passed 4 policemen, and I think it is time the poor boobs wake up. I will let you know more later on, as we feel too good to write very much at present, so hop you will excuse this short note and wish us the best of luck the same as many others. We remind, yours truly, THE BOYS."

While posses scoured the countryside for the Murrells, a newspaper article of a robbery surfaced in Niagara-on-the-Lake. The headline read,"Burglary Near Niagara Frontier May Have Been Work of Escaped Murrells".

According to the paper, the Murrell brothers were believed to have forced an entrance to a drug store in Niagara-on-the-Lake and stolen $2,000 in cash. The previous day they were spotted in Beamsville having breakfast in the Commercial Hotel there. The proprietor of the hotel, when shown a police circular with pictures of the Murrells, positively identified them as his breakfast guests.

Meanwhile police officials from Kitchener responded to a message stating that the Murrell brothers had been captured in Elmira. On their arrival in the village officers discovered a crowd of men, many of them armed, around an old house on the outskirts. Two young men had been captured and another had made his escape. The excited crowd began discussing the reward.

Police soon found that the prisoners were not, in fact, the Murrells. These men hailed from Kitchener and Bridgeport and their names were Clemmer and Lasso. The former had recently been heavily fined for having liquor on his premises. The officials made an inspection of the deserted house and discovered a thoroughly equipped still in operation with a capacity of 25 to 50 gallons a day. There were also 500 pounds of prunes and a large quantity of sugar, all of which were confiscated. Clemmer and Lasso later appeared in police court.

The citizens of Melbourne were furious to hear about the escape of the Murrells. This was one letter to *The London Free Press*:

"It was only with great restraint that the Melbourne citizens kept from meting out some form of punishment to the Murrell brothers upon the day of the hold-up. But, arguing that we have a law in this country which punishes those deserving punishment, the prisoners were not maltreated. We have a law, and we have officers of the law, but of what use? The citizens of Melbourne, unarmed and without police, caught three out of the four bandits and handed them over to the officers of the law, who hadn't the ability to keep them in bondage until tried. A few more instances of such laxity on the part of the law, sir, and we will have irate citizens — and justly irate, too — taking it upon themselves to perform the offices of the law. We will have a system of lynching similar to that of the olden days."

Meanwhile, Henry (Slim) Williams stood trial on robbery charges and received a life sentence to be served at Kingston Penitentiary.

Months passed with no word of the Murrell brothers. Officials believed they had managed to cross the border. Although the media lost interest in the case, the residents of Melbourne still occasionally discussed the escape and the killing of Russell Campbell over morning coffee. It seemed to be a done deed.

1932, Kingston: Wallace Ramesbottom and Henry Quinn were executed for robbery and the murder of city grocer Samuel Weinstein. Ramesbottom was hung on April 26; Quinn was hung on June 24.

Of course this was simply not true. Sydney and William were living in California. Sydney was travelling under the name of "Kid" Brooks, a name taken during a short-lived career as a professional boxer. His luck was about to run out. On the evening of May 2, 1923, Sydney was driving down a road in Nevada when he was stopped by police for having a headlight burned out. The officer quickly discovered that the car had been stolen and arrested Sydney for theft. He was transported to a jail in Susanville, California.

Once again, Sydney attempted to escape — almost successfully. He was then removed to a correctional facility in San Francisco where he was positively identified by the means of fingerprints as the man wanted in London, Ontario. Extradition proceedings were opened and he was subsequently returned to Canada. Sydney was escorted by two Ontario Provincial Police officers to London on July 23.

William Murrell was later discovered residing in California. He was returned to London, Ontario for prosecution purposes and subsequently served a 20 year life sentence for armed robbery.

The trial date was set for the winter with Sydney facing the charge of murder. The crown had proof that a .45 calibre bullet killed Russell Campbell. The only person believed to have handled a colt 45 during the bank heist was Sydney Murrell.

The trial proceedings drew large crowds both inside and out.

At 12:35 p.m. Robert Campbell, brother of the murdered man, was called by the crown. *The London Free Press* reported, "On the stand Robert Campbell told of going towards the bank with the intention of shutting off the motor of the car, which had been left running. He saw two men standing near the bank with revolvers. Passing by the bank he saw his brother Stuart with a rifle in his hand. He went in the bank and followed him. He ran through following the bandits.

"'I heard some shots when I reached the back door and noticed a man running towards the street. I jumped on his back, but he got away. I chased him and with others succeeded in recapturing him. After we caught him I went back into the store and called the doctor, but he was not at home. I then called Dr. Freels of Glencoe and went back and someone told me my brother was dead.' "

During his scuffle in the lane he had noticed a revolver in Sidney Murrell's hand. After the prisoner made his get-away, he rushed down the street and was recaptured, his gun dropping from his hand.

Then Inspector Thomas Nickle testified to Murrell's previous good character. He said he had known the prisoner since he was a small boy and that he had no previous court record. At least not in London.

Additional evidence was offered by Robert E. Campbell (no relation to the deceased), implement agent at Melbourne. According to newspaper accounts, Robert was on his way to his place of business when he saw quite a number of people standing in front of the hotel.

Top left—*The window of the lavatory adjacent to the Murrell's cell, showing the work that had to be performed before a break for liberty. The bars were of heavy iron.*

Top right—*Sidney Murrell (above) and William Murrell. In the background and, left, the jailyard into which the two prisoners dropped from their cell. The ladder is also at left.*

From there they went in the direction of the Home Bank and he followed them, stopping half way between the bank and hotel.

He saw Stewart Campbell and his brother Robert enter the front door of the bank and Russell, who was behind his brother turned into the alley entrance. From his position in front of the hotel he heard two shots fired, presumably in the bank; after a short interval he heard several others fired, possibly four or five after he had arrived half way between the two buildings.

Slim Williams was seen by him to rush out of the alley to the road and Sydney Murrell attempted to follow him when he was grabbed by Robert and Stewart Campbell. In the tussle which followed Stewart Campbell took hold of Sydney Murrell's coat tail and the prisoner turned and pointed a revolver at Stewart Campbell. He saw no more of that incident as he turned and ran after Williams, assisting in his capture.

According to *The London Free Press*, when Sydney Murrell and Slim Williams were tied to the post he alleged that Stewart Campbell said to the former, "You shot my brother."

Murrell in return is alleged to have said "I'm not denying it: I shot five times."

Robert Campbell was asked if there was anything else said?

He replied, "Yes I heard Charlie Long ask, 'Which of you two men did the shooting?' and Sydney Murrell answered: 'I guess I did for I fired five shots.'

"There was also some conversation between the prisoners; this was after William Murrell was brought and placed along with the other two. William Murrell turned to Syd and said: 'Did you do the shooting?' and Syd nodded his head in response.

"Bill said: 'You fool.' Then they whispered to one another and Syd turned to Williams and said: 'Keep quiet and say nothing.'"

Eventually Sydney took the stand. Everyone had waited for this moment. He was asked to explain what happened after his capture. He stated, "On our arrival at London they took us to the police station. We were searched and one or two little things we had were taken away from us.

"Then Detective Downs asked us to identify the revolvers. Slim answered, 'You can tell mine, it has blood on it.'

"William said the other 38 was his and the detective brought the 45 Colt to me and said, 'This is yours.' "

Mr. Donahue for defense then referred to the time when Sydney picking up the 45 revolver from the floor during the bank robbery. He asked, "Where was it before?"

"Norton had it, he asked me for it and I gave it to him," answered Murrell.

At this juncture the cross examination by Mr. Rigney commenced.

Q   "How long did you have it?"

A   "I had it until I threw it away."

Q   "What type of bullets does if fire?"

A   "It is a United States army regulation Colt."

Q   "How is it there were only five shells in it?"

A   "That's all there were in it when I had it."

Q. "And you had fired five shots out of it when you lost it?"

A   "No, I fired three."

Q   "You heard the witnesses in court say you fired five shots. Did you hear anyone ask you if you had shot his brother?"

A   "Yes, I said 'Yes, I'm not denying it'."

Q   "Then you didn't say I fired five shots."

A   "No."

Q   "Do you admit or deny that when you were being chased you tried to fire at them?"

A   "I admit that I tried to fire into the ground to scare them."

Q   "Why did you give your revolver to Norton?"

A   "He asked me for it."

Q   "Didn't he have one?"

A   "Not to my knowledge."

Q   "Did you see him give one to your brother and to Williams?"

A   "No."

Q   "He didn't give you yours?"

A   "No, I brought mine with me."

Q   "And you tell this court and jury that you put your gun into the pocket of a tight-fitting coat?"

A   "Yes."

Q   "Why?"

A   "There was a lot of people around."

Q   "Have you no other explanation to offer?"

A   "No."

Q   "Is that the truth?"

A   "Yes."

Q   "You shot when you were near the open door?"

A   "I'm not sure."

Q   "When it is known that a bullet fitting your gun was taken from the stairway in the alley, what would you say?"

A   "It might be."

Q   "Would it surprise you if that bullet were out of your revolver?"

A   "It is possible it might be."

Q   "It wouldn't surprise you to know that Slim had a 38 calibre, Norton a 38 and your brother a 38?"

A   "I didn't see Norton with a gun."

Q   "You didn't see Norton with a gun?"

A   "No."

Q   "Do you mean to say that you and your brother and Slim and Norton did not display guns the night before when you made arrangements for the robbery?"

A   "No. I only saw three."

Q   "Will you say that Norton did not have a 38?"

A   "I didn't see his gun."

Q   "When did you see the 38 caliber guns?"

A   "The first time was in the bush before we went to the bank."

Q   "When the guns were displayed in the police station here in London, they were all loaded except yours?'

A   "No."

Q   "And your gun in which you had five shells was completely shot
      out?"

A   "I don't know. They did not show us them that way."

Q   "Didn't you know it was empty?"

A   "No."

Q   "You didn't know your gun was no good in a fight?"

A   "Oh. I don't know. A gun like that could be used as a good
      weapon for a club."

Q   "You tried to shoot with the gun?"

A   "Yes."

Q   "And there was no report?"

A   "No.'

Q   "You thought it should have fired?"

A   "Yes, because I thought there were more bullets in it."

Q   "You've heard that a bullet of that size killed Campbell?"

A   "I've heard a witness say that it was a bullet of that size."

Q   "Where did the bullet come from then when you were the only
      man with a .45 caliber gun that we know of?"

A   "Do you mean, Mr. Rigney that I had the only .45?"

Q   "I said do you know where the bullet came from?"

A   "I have no idea."

Q   "Where did you see Russell Campbell?"

A   "I saw a body lying there when I went into the alley."

Q   "The body was lying on the ground?"

A   "Yes, lying flat down, chest to the ground, blood running out of
      the nose. I only got a passing glance, it looked as if it had been
      hit on the face with a brick."

Q   "Then you are telling the truth?"

A   "I am telling what I know as the facts."

"That will do," concluded the crown prosecutor.

Sydney was really in the hot seat. *The London Advertiser* newspaper portrayed the murder of Russell Campbell in this fashion,

Another view of the London jail.

"Unarmed, Russell Campbell rushed to the side door and found himself face to face with one of the thugs who immediately began firing, discharging five cartridges. One of the shots got Campbell just below the heart, penetrating both lungs. It was found to be .45 calibre revolver bullet. His brother, Robert Campbell, who followed close on his heels, grappled with the bandit, but the latter threw him to the earth. Then a third brother, Stuart Campbell, grabbed the stranger's coat-tail, while another citizen tripped him. A crowd eagerly assisted in his capture."

The London Free Press emphasized the disorganization of the murder investigation when they wrote, "W. H. Stringer, Inspector of the Criminal Investigation Department of the Ontario provincial police, who conducted a search here some time ago for the clothes of the murdered man, is understood to be one of the additional witnesses. Neither the clothes which the murdered man wore on the day of the shooting nor the bullet which killed him have been recovered, according to the most authentic information."

On February 5, Sidney was found guilty of murder by the jury. He was sentenced by Judge Lennox on February 9th to be hanged by the neck until dead.

Did Sydney Murrell really shoot and kill Russell Campbell? Did Pat Norton own a .45 calibre revolver? Was Pat Norton actually the first to leave the bank by way of the alleyway? If so, he would have encountered Russell Campbell. Gun shots were heard coming from where Russell stood. Sydney did state that while escaping he came across Campbell lying on the ground. However, only one .45 Colt was found missing five bullets. Sydney under oath declared that he had only shot three bullets. Is it possible when Norton borrowed Sidney's gun that he fired two shots, killing Campbell, and then discarded the gun in the bank before fleeing? We may never know.

Sydney Murrell was buried in an unmarked grave in a London cemetery, thanks to a friend of the family who had kindly donated a gravesite in their family plot. Murderers were not allowed to be buried in holy ground.

The Murrell family have suffered the shame of Sidney's death by hanging. Some family members strongly believed he never committed murder. There were too many unanswered questions, too many illogical events, too many circumstantial conclusions. There are still family alive who pray to clear the family name one day.

An Alternative to Divorce in Port Hope

*L*ove is a potent tonic. One sip leads to another and another and another. It is so potent it can justify any action - even murder. Could a man poison his own wife to quench this thirst? Perhaps John Reginald Hooper did.

On the morning of October 6, 1893, a crowd gathered outside the residence of Joseph Hooper in Port Hope, Ontario. Three men emerged from the house. One was Chief of Police John Douglas, the second, Constable Jarvis, and the third was John Reginald Hooper, son of Joseph Hooper. John was handcuffed and escorted to a carriage. Despite his pallor, John gave a military salute to the crowd with his free hand. Was it true what the gossip said he did? No, it couldn't be, not John Hooper!

John was well-known in town; he had been born in Port Hope and learned the printing trade in the newspaper office of *The Guide*. He also served for some years in the military, "A" Battery, first in Kingston and then in Quebec. While in Quebec he met and married a French-Canadian girl, Georgiana Leblanc, from St. Ambrose de Kildare. The couple settled in Ottawa, where John entered the civil service in 1887 as a clerk in the Post Office Department. Does he sound like a murder suspect yet?

The Port Hope Weekly of October 13, 1893, described Mr. Hooper's dilemma: "Port Hope is in a matter of excitement over rather peculiar circumstances surrounding the death of the wife of John R. Hooper. Hooper has been engaged at the Post Office Department at Ottawa. For the last two years his wife was an inmate of the Insane Asylum at Kingston. The facts as near as known are that Hooper took his wife from the Asylum on September 10th having the order of the Superintendent to do so. He took her to Montreal, and subsequently while travelling on a train she jumped off at Louiseville and almost drowned in the river. Hooper found her again all right, and on the 18th, while again on a train, she was taken ill, and at Terrebonne near Montreal, was removed to the station and died.

"Hooper conveyed the body to Port Hope, where his relatives reside, and the body was buried without any funeral services, in a cemetery out of town. The actions of Hooper in all the transactions were so peculiar, that the body was exhumed last week and the stomach sent to Toronto for analysis. Should poison be found in the stomach, undoubtedly the position will be bad for Hooper. At present the evidence tends to the impression that Hooper's wife being a confined maniac, he practically had not a wife. He had formed an attachment for a young woman in Ottawa, who supposed him to be a widower."

Action began immediately after John buried his wife and returned to Ottawa. He seemed confident and relaxed. The telegraph operator at a C.P.R. station near Montreal changed all that. Upon hearing of the death, he recalled that the woman's male companion had called himself Cooper, and that a man of that same name had recently sent a telegram from his office to the agent at Louiseville asking him to look out for a 'crazy woman'. After some discussion with the conductor of the train he took his story to the police because he thought the death should be investigated.

The *Montreal Witness* newspaper scooped this most sensational story and ran it in their September 22 issue, "Intense excitement was created at the Central Folloe Station this morning by the report of suburban murder. The following weird story was told by a telegraph operator, who works at a station near Montreal.

"While on duty on Monday evening a man came into the office and handed him a message which was addressed to the agent at Louiseville and which read as follows: 'Look out for crazy woman.'

"A few hours later the man returned and asked the operator to ask Louiseville if anything had been seen of the crazy woman. Nothing seen yet.

"The stranger said he was very anxious to get an answer as he was leaving on the 5:15 p.m. train for Jolliette. Just before the train left he told the operator to send the answer to him on board the Jollette train somewhere on the line.

"About 6:30 p.m. the agent at Louiseville called up the operator and asked if the women's name was Georgiana, if so, she had been found. He answered back 'That is the party.' I also told the agent to telegraph the stranger on the Jolliette train and ask him what he wanted to do with the woman, which he did.

"On Wednesday the operator happened to meet the stranger, who said his name was Cooper. He said he had not received a message from Louiseville, but assured the operator that everything had been just fine.

"'After I left Cooper,' continued the operator, 'I learned that on the Monday evening in question a woman had been taken suddenly ill on the Quebec train near Terrebonne. A male companion was with her at the time. He took the woman off at Terrebonne station where she expired in a few moments. The man with her was asked his name and he replied that it was McDonald, but later said it was Cooper.'

"The body remained at Terrebonne all that night and was put on the Jolliette train on the following morning by the man McDonald or Cooper, who said he was going to take it to Port Hope."

> 1834, Perth: John Wilson shot and killed Robert Lyon in the last duel fought in Canada on June 13, 1833. The duel was fought over a woman, Elizabeth Hughes. In June of 1834 he was acquitted and he moved to London from Toronto where he took on a law practice. He and Elizabeth were subsequently married.

The paper also related to the telegraph operator's story. "Before the body left on the Toronto train Conductor Robitaille of the Quebec train came to me and said he was on the train when the woman was taken so mysteriously ill and died so suddenly. He said that just before the train reached Terrebonne he noticed the man who was with the woman give her something to drink which looked like milk. Soon after drinking it she was taken very ill, becoming worse till the end at Terrebonne. The conductor said the woman did not look or act as if she was crazy."

Soon other papers picked up the story and it became the scandal of the day. Silas Carpenter, a government detective, was assigned to the case.

On September 28th, Hooper sent a telegram to the *Editors Times Guide*, in Port Hope, hoping to dispell any rumours. It stated, "Please publish denial of report regarding death of Mrs. Hooper. She had attempted her own life twice, but was stopped by her husband. Am writing, J.R. Hooper."

Hooper aroused suspicion when he returned to Port Hope the next day and proceeded to have his wife's body exhumed, with the intention of having it embalmed. The opening of the grave was in progress when the undertaker, J.T. George insisted that it was illegal without a coroner's order. Hooper promptly requested Dr. Corbett, the coroner, to hold an inquest. He agreed to do this once approval was granted by the County Crown Attorney. What was Hooper attempting to conceal?

Community interest soared when it was announced that there would be a coroner's inquest. The jury was composed of 20 well-known Port Hope citizens, crowds gathered at the railway station to catch sight of the witnesses arriving from Montreal and elsewhere; people clamoured for access to the Opera House where the inquest was to be held.

A number of Port Hope residents were interviewed and speculation began to grow after testimony from Dr. Clarke, Superintendent of the Rockwood Asylum in Kingston. Other witnesses included the conductor of the train on which the alleged crime was committed, the druggist who sold Hooper prussic acid and Miss Stapley, the other woman in the case.

The Crown was represented by C. A. Cornellier, Q.C., for the province of Quebec and J.W. Kerr, Q.C., and W. F. Kerr, of Cobourg, the Ontario government and Mr. H. A. Ward plied the defense for Mr. Hooper. Coroner Corbett presided over the court.

Robert Webb, a druggist from Montreal testified, "I remember Sunday 17th of September last. Dr. Cameron issued an order which read as follows: 'Let bearer have enough hydrocyanic acid to poison a large dog.' Dr. Cameron lives on McGill College Ave. in Montreal. I am conversant with his signature. The bearer of this order came in about 3:30 p.m. on Sunday afternoon. Hooper asked me to be sure to give him enough to kill a large dog as it was a favorite and the owner of the dog wanted it killed speedily, and did not want to see the poor dog suffer. The dog was going mad and was muzzled. He asked how it had better be administered. I suggested putting it in a tin of water. I gave him hydrocyanic acid, commonly called prussic acid. He received half an ounce in liquid form.

"I did not think of the matter until I saw a paragraph in the *Star* about three weeks later headed 'Hooper and the doctor.' I then went to Dr. Cameron. The doctor was not in but I met him on the street. He said he was satisfied that it was the same order given to Hooper. The quantity of acid given would fill an ordinary tablespoon. It was a two per cent solution. There was enough to kill a large dog and enough to kill a person."

It would seem that one good potion deserves another.

Mrs. Joseph Cooper of Port Hope was the next witness called, "I am well acquainted with John R. Hooper; have known him from a boy. Was acquainted with the late Mrs. John R. Hooper. Think it was in 1885. She boarded with me then. Her husband was in the Northwest at the time, during the rebellion. She came to my house alone. Her husband came to my house on his return. There was nothing wrong in particular with her as to her health, and she was a lady, so far as I know by her actions.

"John R. Hooper called on the afternoon of the day of the burial. I asked for his wife; he said she was buried that morning. I said I was sorry, as I would have liked to have seen her, and he said that he had a funeral service down below (in Quebec). His wife wished to die a Protestant. He also said the deceased's mother was a fine lady, and left it to him as to burial, and told him to remove the remains

> 1872: Phoebe Campbell was convicted of killing her husband, George, with an axe. She was hanged June 20, the only woman to be hanged in Middlesex County. The executioner refused to hang her so the sheriffs recruited a prisoner to perform the hanging. Commemorative postcards were issued afterward.

before one of the other relatives should interfere. Hooper stated that she had suffered for two years from cancer of the womb. She had undergone an operation, but would not take chloroform. He did not mention the time when the operation took place. He was excited. He told me that he had started from below Quebec for Montreal. He said he had placed her in a Pullman car in an easy chair and she turned very pale just after doing so, and gave a groan; think he said he went for a drink, but am not sure; she gave another groan and rose erect on her feet and died in his arms in the car. He made no mention of his wife having been in an asylum. He said she might have been a little insane from the effects of a cancer."

The next witness was the mysterious woman Miss Alice Stapley or better known by newspaper accounts as 'the other woman'.

"Leblanc - At Lille, France, on the 1st, Georgiana, youngest daughter of the late Oliver Leblanc and Delice St. Andre, wife of John R. Hooper, aged 20 years and 8 months."

Here was John Hooper's dangerous sip of love's elixir! What had that done to him?

"I am acquainted with John R. Hooper since the latter part of April last. I went to Montreal on the 8th, Hooper was at the station to see me off, my mother was with me. He said he would try to get his vacation as soon as he could, he said he would ask to get off the next day (Saturday). He said he intended to spend part of his vacation with his sister in Port Hope.

"I next saw Mr. Hooper on the following Monday, September 11th. I said I was surprised to see him, did not think to see him so soon. He said he had been at Kingston. I did not ask how he went or how he came to Montreal. I saw Hooper again before he called, think it was on Wednesday (September 13th). He said he had come from Louiseville. We went to Windsor station, my grandmother came in by C.P.R. He said he left something at Louiseville and had to go back, think he said it was a valise or cloak, am not sure if he said what it was. The next time I saw him he called at my brother-in-law's house on Thursday. He called on Friday. I next saw Hooper on the following day (Saturday) and Sunday. He told me he was going out of town on the following Monday to see his sister at Port Hope. This was Sunday, September 17. I am sure that it was on the following day that he was going to see his sister. He said he would call on his return; did not say how long he expected to be absent.

"I saw him on September 24, the last Sunday I was in Montreal. On Monday we took the train that afternoon for Ottawa.

"I did receive three letters from Hooper while in Montreal. In one of them from Louiseville he said, 'You will be surprised to hear I am here.' He said something about passing the time at the mineral springs.

"He had not proposed marriage before going to Montreal. He proposed marriage the last Saturday I was there. He had been coming off and on during the summer. He had often said that he thought the same of me as a sister. I said, in reply to his proposal, if my parents were willing for me to marry him I was. I made my father and mother acquainted with this proposal. I heard that he had been married, and asked him if it were true, and he said his wife was dead. He told me this early in the summer, a month or two after I first met him. I asked how long she had been dead; he replied over a year. He was coming frequently to our house at this time. I did not question him concerning his former wife, as I understood it hurt his feelings. This last fall he said that his first wife had been in an asylum before she died. He said she died in France."

According to Miss Stapley Mr. Hooper during the summer had taken a death notice from his pocket. She added, "He often, after that, said his wife was dead. I believed him."

Love's potion had done a strong job as the following newspaper clipping will identify. It was read in court by the coroner:

Miss Stapley continued her testimony, "I received one letter from Mrs. Baulch from Port Hope with a note from Mr. Hooper after Hooper left me that last time I saw him at Ottawa. The letter stated he was sick at his father's home, and not to believe false reports. When it was reported to me that John R. Hooper's wife had died on the train I thought there was a mistake."

Dr. Douglas, of Cobourg, and Dr. Corbett, Jr., made the post mortem examination and filed a shared report in detail on the condition of the various organs of the body of the late Mrs. J.R. Hooper.

"We did not open the spinal column except that portion visible, the brain and upper portion of the spinal cord were pale in colour. The arteries were empty and the blood vessels at the base of the brain were all empty except small portions on the right side of the head. So far as we could judge all the vital organs of the body were normal and healthy. After having examined the brain, heart, spinal column, liver, stomach, kidneys, bladder and womb it is not possible to account for death in any natural cause. There was no cancer of the womb, there was no disease of the heart, all organs were healthy."

Professor W.H. Ellis of Toronto also studied the stomach and concluded, "I found no poison nor anything which throws any light on the cause of death. I found the stomach tied at both ends, but empty, would consider it a healthy organ.

"Prussic acid two percent in doses of about less than one dram is fatal. It is one of the most rapid poisons known, it is very volatile. There are cases when it could not be detected after twenty four hours and it has been detected after days, and even weeks.

"In the absence of traces of poison and with the symptoms, the fact of traces of poison not being found in this case is not proof that death did not occur from prussic acid poisoning."

At the close of the evidence the Hall was cleared of all lawyers and press representatives, and the witnesses. The jury's deliberations were long and heated.

The following is the verdict arrived at: "That the said Georgiana Leblanc Hooper came to her death on the 18th September last at Terrebonne station, Quebec, under suspicious circumstances from causes unknown to this jury."

This was not an end but a new beginning; John Reginald Hooper was arrested on a warrant charging him with the murder of his wife through the administration of prussic acid. He was escorted to Jolliette, Quebec to stand trial.

During this time Detective Carpenter focused his investigations on the events leading up to the death of Georgiana Hooper. Carpenter visited Mrs. Leblanc, the mother-in-law of Hooper who lived in

St. Ambroise de Kildare, and her parish priest. He appropriated some very significant facts. He learned that Hooper had visited the priest shortly before his wife's death. Hooper needed a permit to transfer his wife to the asylum at Verdum but told the priest that the woman was no relation to him and that the parish would be responsible for her keep in the asylum. The priest discovered that the woman was actually his wife and refused the permit. Hooper's next attempt at a permit was Mayor Neveux, of St. Ambroise de Kildare. This too failed. Hooper needed his wife to disappear—forever. He wanted his freedom and he was getting desperate.

Carpenter also found out that Hooper had used several names and identities during this time. The telegrams he sent were all signed differently. Hooper had told conductor Robitaille of the C.P.R. that he was a government employee charged to find, confine and accompany "crazy" people to asylums. The pseudonyms he used were Macdonald and Cooper.

How far did he or would he go for his next sip of love's elixir?

The trial began on January 3, 1893. Officials believed it would last two weeks. A journalist for *The Port Hope Evening Guide* reported, "Hooper looked a little pale today, but seems confident of the result. When Hooper was called to the dock he ascended the steps in a confident manner, and nodded brightly to his lawyers. For a man who is on trial for his life, he certainly is showing remarkable confidence. The prisoner was allowed to be seated during the trial."

Dr. Corbett of Port Hope was the first to be called and was asked to produce the bottles of embalming fluid that he had found to be in Hooper's possession while he was exhuming his wife's body at the gravesite at Port Hope.

Dr. Chas. Clarke, Medical Superintendent of Rockwood Insane Asylum of Kingston testified next. He informed the jury that Hooper had brought his wife to the asylum on October 14th, 1891 and registered her as Georgiana Hooper. The application stated that she was not subject to fits, and that she had never attempted to injure either herself or others. Hooper wrote a letter to Clarke soon thereafter to inquire if his wife was displaying violence. A reply to Hooper stated that her condition was much the same as when admitted, that she was very excitable, but that her case should be a hopeful one.

Dr. Clarke explained that although Georgina enjoyed good health during her stay, she refused to take much food at first, as she imagined it was poisoned. During her stay she was always cheerful, and willing to do any work the asylum authorities gave her to do.

Sometime during the summer Dr. Clarke received a letter from Hooper asking to take his wife to Europe with him where she could be with her mother. On August 7th, he was told that he could take his wife away any time he desired.

On September 11, 1893 at approximately 4 a.m., Hooper picked his wife up and boarded a ship bound for Montreal.

The Crown then asked Dr. Clarke if she ever complained of cancer?

He replied, "No, never."

Herbert Holden, the steward on the steamer Algerian, was the first witness in the afternoon session. Holden testified that on September 10th, Hooper and his wife had indeed boarded the steamer Algerian. Sometime later he saw them in the salon, where she was playing the piano. He told them to stop. Hooper replied that the woman was crazy, and that he was a guard taking her to Montreal.

The first witness for the defense was Mrs Leblanc, mother of Georgina Hooper. She testified as follows:

"I am seventy years of age. In September last my son Edmund Leblanc came for me and took me to the Hotel Rivard at Jolliette to see my son-in-law, Mr. Hooper. He told me that his wife had thrown herself into the river at Louiseville. He seemed to be very sorry and was crying and asked for help to go look for her. My son Edmund went down with him. Mr. Hooper said that she had thrown herself off the car into the water. He showed me a piece of paper with something written on it. But I could not read. Hooper told me in English that it said, 'Good bye, John, good bye: I am going to destroy myself.'

"The same evening they came back with Georgiana and left her at my house for a few days. They told us to take good care of her and he would pay us well. She remained there for fives days and slept and ate very little. Once she went out to the spring and got water and washed herself all over. The next morning she went into the garden and picked flowers, barefooted and bareheaded, when it was raining. She did have many lucid moments during the five days she was at my house. She thought she was God and had to suffer death for sins. She said that she had thrown herself into the river to save the world. She never said that John had thrown her into the river. I have had twenty-four children. When Georgiana left my place she said she felt that she would never reach town alive."

Mrs. Leblanc fainted at this point. Several doctors in the courtroom rushed to give her medical assistance and she revived and proceeded with her evidence.

"Whenever I saw them together he treated her kindly and they seemed to be happy."

Georgiana's mother returned to the stand the following day. This time her words caused a stir in the courtroom. By her account on the Sunday evening preceding Georgiana's death, when the latter was playing and singing at the piano, a bird came to the window pane. Georgiana said, "It is my late sister Josephine who has come for me; I am going to die."

The following morning Georgiana went out into the garden, saying that she was going to dig her grave, as by six o'clock that evening she would be dead. She spent two hours digging in the earth with her fingers.

When Hooper took her away he said that he was going to take

> 1873, Oxford County: Timothy Topping, a west Oxford farmer, went berserk and killed his wife and four of his eight children. Topping was the Assessor and Tax Collector for the county. One Sunday morning Topping used an axe to chop the heads off his children. His wife attempted to interfere and he gave her the chop as well. He then grabbed a knife and slit his own throat but he lived to stand trial. The scene of the crime was open to the public and several people took advantage of this to enter the house and view the bodies. At his trial the jury decided Topping was insane and committed him to the London Asylum. Once again he went berserk and in a scuffle with a guard, he was clubbed to death.

her to a place where she would be well taken care of and that her mother need not worry about her.

In the cross examination by M.J.A. Renaud the distraught mother broke down in tears. She admitted that she did not know any of the circumstances around the jump from the train nor did she know her daughter had been in an asylum in Kingston.

She added, "I am sure that Hooper told me at the Hotel Rivard that his wife had attempted to commit suicide."

Renaud then asked, "If you were so sure that your daughter was so dangerously ill while at your house why did you not go for a doctor?"

She replied, "I felt that no doctor could ever do her good. I felt she was going to die and doctors cannot bring dead people back to life. When my daughter left with Hooper she was not stouter than a skeleton."

Mr. Ophile Duval, an employee of the Notre Dame Hospital was next on the stand.

According to Duval, Hooper brought his wife to the hospital on September 11. She was placed in room 506, on the pay ward and Dr. Marsolais attended her. She was taken away about ten o'clock the following night by Hooper.

In the hospital Hooper gave his name as Cooper. He said he was not related to this woman but was taking care of her to oblige some of her relatives.

He wanted her to stay at the hospital until he could place her in an asylum. He did not enter any name on the hospital register.

Dr. A. R. Marsolais of the Notre Dame Hospital provided sensational evidence next. He said the prisoner brought the deceased woman to the hospital on Monday, September 11; the doctor examined the woman and found that she was quite insane. Hooper then requested a certificate of insanity and the doctor gave him one. Hooper also told the doctor that he was not related to her.

The doctor saw Hooper again on September 15, at his private office, where Hooper told him of his trouble with her when she had jumped off the train, but that he had eventually got her home. He said her parents wanted her to be placed in an asylum. Hooper then produced an asylum form which he wanted filled in. The name used according to the doctor was Cooper.

He wanted her placed as a 'person without means'. He asked for the certificate to read that the deceased lived in Montreal instead of St. Ambroise. Hooper at this time said the deceased was a prostitute but when the doctor said she did not look like one he asked her to be entered as a pauper. The doctor did not comply.

The testimony to this point would seem to imply that Hooper wished to hide his wife away with no connection to himself and thereby have the freedom to marry Miss Stapley. The next two witnesses, however, Selina Downs and Mrs. Frank Martin, provided a new possibility, a wild card for the game of love and death. Did Georgiana Hooper have a death wish? Did she, in fact, poison herself on the train?

Selina Downs, stated, "Prisoner and his wife boarded with me from October 17, 1887, until March 15, 1888. During that time Mr. Hooper was very kind to his wife. She had attacks of hysteria three times during their stay at my place. She screamed, fell on the floor and set her teeth. She remained in the fit about twenty minutes. My husband tried to open her teeth once to give her water, but could not. She was very bad tempered. Once when her husband insisted on going out in the evening she hit him on the mouth and then left the tea table and went upstairs, where she threw herself on the floor. She was always sick after these attacks. The third time she got angry at me for something I said to her, she fell where she was. I never spoke to anyone about these fits except to my husband, until to-day."

The following spring the Hoopers' boarded with Mrs. Frank Martin who testified "In the spring of 1888 the accused and his wife boarded with me. One day she told me that she had drunk a bottle of ink to try and poison herself and had been very sick after it. She said she would buy poison later on."

It would seem this case was more complicated than first thought. The jury had an unenviable task.

The most intriguing segment of the trial was about to begin. Did Georgiana Hooper attempt suicide by throwing herself off the train and into the river? Or was it her husband who pushed her and attempted to drown her?

The jury first heard from Gustave Doucet, a telegraph operator who was on vacation in Louiseville on September 12th of 1893. At about three o'clock in the afternoon Hooper walked into the hotel when he encountered Doucet. He said he was in search of a woman twenty-four years of age, who had run away from St. Ambroise de Kildare, and as she was pretty and out of her mind, he was concerned for her well-being. He also inquired if there was a telegraph office at St. Ambroise de Kildare. Doucet checked and found there was none. During their conversation Hooper said he was from Toronto, but had been in Ottawa for a day; he then asked about the rivers near there. The telegraph operator informed him of two rivers, one larger than the other in the direction of Quebec City.

When Hooper asked the way to the station, Doucet decided to accompany him there and then they went by the river and the bridge. After noting the rapid current they returned to the station.

It was about 5 o'clock in the afternoon and Hooper boarded the train to Montreal.

Philippe Bellefeuille, conductor of the Canadian Pacific Railway, saw Hooper on the train leaving Montreal on the night of September 12th. Bellefeuille explains what he saw, "There was a crazy woman with him. They had two second class tickets from Montreal to Three Rivers and rode in a colonial car. There were five or six other passengers in the car. She was quiet."

Bellefeuille saw them in the train as far as Louiseville, but after that they disappeared. His train was due at Louiseville at 1:46 a.m. the morning of September 13. There were stations between Louiseville and Three Rivers and the distance between was 21 miles. The conductor saw no baggage with the couple on the train and there was none checked.

Cleophas Boduc, the brakeman, on board Bellefeuille's train, corroborated the evidence. When he entered the car the woman winked at him and he winked back. Surely there was no harm in that?

Another brakeman, named Pierre Morin, testified to seeing Hooper and his wife get off his train at Louiseville on that very same night in September. Morin stated, "Hooper got off on the opposite side to the station and said to me, 'Never mind us, go inside.' He and the woman were standing side by side. I could not say which of the two jumped off first. The train was still slightly moving when they leaped off. I heard no cry. They seemed to get off voluntarily."

The train then remained at the station long enough to take on water.

The Desauiniers' family lived just down the river from the Louiseville railway bridge. At 2:55 a.m. on Wednesday September 13, Mrs. Desauiniers was awakened by a knock at the front door. Opening the door she was greeted by a weeping woman whose wet hair hung in a disordered manner about her neck and shoulders. The poor creature was soaking wet.

The Port Hope Weekly Guide continues the tale, "She told Mrs. Desauiniers that some dark man had thrown her from the bridge and tried to drown her. The reason she had not been drowned she said, was because she had floated to shore and had saved herself by catching hold of some bushes near shore. She told the people if the dark man came for her to be sure and tell him that she was not there. She often mentioned a man named John, but did not mention his other name."

According to Conductor E.R.R. Bitaille, Hooper boarded the train at Louiseville for Montreal on the morning of the 13th of September, and requested that Bitaille send a message to all the agents along the line asking them to look out for a crazy woman. Bitaille stated that Hooper represented himself as a government agent for the insane, and then slept quietly for the balance of the night.

On September 14, Hooper was notified that Georgiana had been found and was housed at the Desauiniers' home. Hooper and his brother-in-law Edmond travelled to Louiseville to take charge of Mrs Hooper.

According to Mrs. Desauiniers, Hooper sent Edmond in first. As soon as Mrs Hooper saw her brother she was greatly pleased and inquired about her parents. Mrs. Desauinier asked Edmond who Hooper was and if he too had come for the woman.

Edmond quietly explained that Hooper had told him not to tell what relation he was to the woman. He asked Mrs. Desauiniers not to betray him as Hooper had been very good to his family and had often given them money, and did not want that to change.

Mrs. Desauiniers then invited Hooper into the house. He seemed stiff and uncomfortable. Nonetheless, when Georgiana saw her husband she appeared pleased and kissed him, but he was so cool with her that she became very angry and said she had a secret to tell.

Mrs. Desauiniers stated that when Hooper saw how angry she was he petted her until she became calm again. Mrs. Desauiniers generously served them all dinner although Hooper insisted that he and his wife be served in different rooms. After dinner they headed back to Georgiana's parent's home.

The Port Hope Weekly summarized the case for the prosecution thus, "On Monday evening, September 11, it will be shown that Hooper took a train alone for Louiseville, via Jolliette, where he arrived on Tuesday morning at 2 a.m., and began to make enquiries about the crazy woman. He is supposed to have arrived in Montreal on Tuesday night, and left the same night on the Quebec train with Mrs. Hooper for her home, but instead of getting off at Lanorale, the nearest station to her home, he got off at Louiseville, lost her, and an hour later took a train for Montreal from Louiseville alone. When he got on the train he telegraphed the agents to look out for a crazy woman. He arrived in Montreal on Wednesday morning, September 13. On September 14, he heard that his wife has been found and that she claimed to have been thrown by someone into a river. He went for her with his brother-in-law and brought her on a freight train to Lanorale and from there drove her to her home at St. Ambroise de Kildare, where he left her till Monday, September 18, when he returned for her, and after failing to get a permit to put her in an insane asylum put her on a train at Lanorale with his brother-in-law. When the train reached Masoonche he told his brother-in-law that he can return home. Then he took her into the baggage car and before she reached Terreboone, the next station, she fell on the floor of the car and expired at Terrebonne station."

Conductor Robitalle was the last person other than Hooper to see Georgiana alive. His testimony helped to cast doubt on Hooper's innocence, but would it be enough to convict him?

Robitalle stated, "Prisoner asked me if he could be allowed to take his wife into the baggage car and I consented. His wife appeared to be in good health. The train stopped at Masoouche for about two minutes, and, waving my lamp to the engineer to go ahead, I turned around and saw the prisoner pouring something down his wife's throat out of a tin cup. I said to him, 'Don't pour water into her mouth, you will choke her.' He replied, 'I am moistening her lips, as the doctor told me to do.'

"Her mouth was twisted and I saw froth coming from it. She never uttered a sound. Her body was perfectly limp. Her eyes were large and glassy."

As they pulled into Terrebonne station tankman Duguay carried Mrs. Hooper from the car into the station and there she died.

As for the tin cup, it was left in the baggage car and approximately 55 minutes later the conductor rinsed the cup and used it to take a drink.

January 19th saw the end of the trial. The jury had heard sixty witnesses. Was John Hooper guilty of the murder of his wife? The jury said no. His acquittal was largely based on the contradictory nature of the medical evidence, on which he was given the benefit of the doubt.

Nevertheless, he was not permitted to go free. He was immediately re-arrested and this time he was charged with the attempted murder of his wife by drowning. This time he was to be tried at Three Rivers, Quebec.

On June 5, 1894, John Reginald Hooper appeared in the Court of Queen's Bench at Three Rivers. Judge Bourgeois presided. Hooper was arraigned and asked for his plea. Raising his hands he called God and man to witness that he was not guilty of any crime. Judge Bourgeois abruptly interrupted the prisoner and informed him in very plain language that all he had to do was to say whether he was guilty or not.

"Well, I am not guilty, then," answered Hooper, as he calmly adjusted the flower on the lapel of his coat.

Following adjournment Hooper stayed in the box a few minutes, and shook hands with anyone who wanted to shake hands with him.

"I will come and see you again before Friday," said the Anglican minister, and he shook hands with Hooper.

"Why, of course, come and see me just as often as you wish. You will always find me at home. I am not one of those men who go abroad much, you know. You are always sure to find me in," Hooper replied laughingly.

It was thought that there would be upwards of forty witnesses present for this trial. The cost of trying Hooper was escalating into the thousands of dollars. Some stated it neared $40,000 at this time.

Once again the witnesses were called to testify and once again the stories remained the same as in Jolliette. On June 16, John Reginald Hooper awaited the decision of the court. The verdict rendered stated that John Reginald Hooper was guilty of attempting to drown his wife. At 2:30 p.m. the Clerk of the Crown read the conviction and asked Hooper if he had anything to say as to why the sentence should not be passed according to law.

The Port Hope paper recorded his response, "One of the most remarkable harangues ever uttered in a court of justice in this Province was then given by John Reginald Hooper. He spoke for three hours and a half, giving reasons why sentence should not be passed upon him. His language, at times, was violent, as was his manner. His remarks as to how he had been tried were scathing.

"This afternoon, for the first time, John Reginald Hooper stands in the dock without a bouquet in the lapel of his coat.

"Fully one thousand people are packed together like sardines in the court room, in the corridors and on the stairs, while nearly as many more are gathered outside to catch a glimpse of Hooper."

Hooper's speech was a brilliant and a convincing attempt to escape his fate. This is what he said, "I want this court to grant me a new trial as my trial has not been a fair one. If I had wanted to get a divorce from my wife I could have got one for $10, but instead of doing that, I paid for her support in the asylum like a loving husband. Now, the reason why I took my wife from the Kingston Asylum was to put her in the asylum at Longue Pointe. There was no harm in that. I took her to the Notre Dame Hospital because I had nowhere else to take her. She was violent there and the nuns told me that she disturbed the other patients.

"At last they consented to keep her there one day, and no longer. I could not place her in any hotel, and my great fear was that the papers would get hold of it and make a sensation out of it, as all my friends thought.

"Place yourself in my position and see the trouble I was in. Through exposure during the rebellion I suffered from rheumatism and Dr. Cousins, of Ottawa, advised me to go to St. Leon or Caledonia Springs. My wife had been twice to St. Leon Springs with Mrs. Lemay, of Montreal. Louiseville is the nearest station to St. Leon Springs.

"So I took her by a round about way to the train. I had a parcel and a small valise. I know not what was in the parcel, except that one of the ladies at the hospital said a wrapper was in it. A great deal of stress was laid on the fact of my taking my wife down by second class car. Would any one else have done otherwise with an insane woman, who used vile language?

"I do not see why those railway men persecute me. The two brakesmen were not in the car ten minutes altogether. On the way the names of the stations were called. I wanted to go to Three Rivers, and when she heard Louiseville called, she ran to the door and got out on the platform. I then made up my mind to put her in the baggage car when the train stopped, but she jumped before it stopped. I caught her by the gossamer cloak that she wore, but it gave way. She fell and rolled over two or three times. I jumped after her and fell on my side. I caught her, and while the train was at the station put her back on the step. If Bolduc saw me at all it was then — as I was trying to get her in. I told Dunn my hat blew off; it was true. It did blow off and as I turned she jumped again. It was a dark night and I could not see her. I do not know what became of her for I never saw her again. I thought she must have gone in the direction of Montreal. So I boarded the next train to look for her. She could run like a deer and I was crippled up with rheumatism.

"I wish to God now, that I had stayed at Louiseville. My intention was then to get off at Maskinonge, but the conductor told me that the station was closed and that there was no operator there. I want to say before God I never was east of the station at Louiseville that night. When I heard that there was nobody at Maskinonge, I resolved to go to Jolliette. There is only one train a day, and I was obliged to go to Montreal or elsewhere to wait for the other train which would have taken me there no sooner. The first thing I did was to send the telegrams all along the line.

"About that death notice of my wife, which I handed to Miss Stapley, of Ottawa, who put that in the papers I do not know, but when I saw it I cut it out, and when Miss Stapely asked me if I was a married man I handed it to her. You ask me why I handed it to her. I did so before God to save her honor. It is true that I told Dr. Marsolais that my wife was a prostitute, and I regret to say that it was true. But I never thought the doctor would repeat what I told him privately, in evidence against me. It is true that I told lies and said the woman was not my wife. I did that because I was ashamed to be seen in company with an insane woman.

"If I had looked longer for her the Crown would have had no case against me. I can say that witnesses have been paid by the Crown to swear falsely against me. I swear before God that my wife wrote those words on the paper that she was going to drown. The reporters have lied against me, why? Because they made a fat thing out of the case. The officers of the Crown have also made a fat thing out of the case. No wonder they wanted to drag out the case as long as they could. To convict me the Crown has had to spend nearly $40,000, and the poor people will be taxed to pay this. I have been persecuted from the first. I was brought down into a French country to be tried, and eleven of the jurors who tried me spoke the French language. No wonder I was found guilty. If I had been a Frenchman I would have got off all right. Why was I not tried by Protestants? If I had been tried in Ontario the verdict would have been a different one, I see over your Honor's head the words, 'God and my right.' You should take that down and write, 'The end justifies the means.'

"When I was taken to Jolliette, C.A. Cornillier, Q.C., came to me at the dead of night and demanded admission in the name of the Attorney-General. The Chief of Police, Mr. Leduc, an honorable man, informed my lawyers of it. Why did he visit me at the dead of night?

"He told me he represented the Attorney-General and that it was in his power to keep me or let me off.

"Ten minutes later he returned and said that money would do the thing, leaving me under the impression that if I paid him he would set me free. In the morning I was told that if I paid $300 I would be let go. The visit was brought up and stated in the papers that he intimidated me by saying that he had evidence enough to hang me.

"That is how I was treated in this Province. The race and religion cry was raised against me. My letters were opened by the Crown in order to convict me. That was a damnable deed.

"Oh, yes, I have been cruelly treated. There will be such a howl raised over Ontario and this Province if I am not granted a new trial that never before was heard of. The means the Crown has taken to convict me, I say, would not be allowed in darkest Russia or Spain. Your honor told the jury that if they found that I had neglected to take care of my wife after I took her off the train that I was just as guilty as if I had thrown her into the river. Do you call this British law? I call it French law. It was cruel, cruel to say that. Hear what the Bible says, 'Let him that is without sin cast the first stone, and they went away and left her.'

1890, Henry James Smith was convicted of beating his wife to death with the family Bible. On the scaffold Smith confessed that the woman had not been his real wife, who he had apparently deserted in England, 30 years earlier.

"Some twenty years ago a man was hung in this very town who was innocent. I swear I am not guilty. I have not had British fair play.

"The people of Port Hope believed I was innocent and sent a petition asking for prompt trial or admission to bail. The Attorney-General regretted his inability to do so.

"The law distinctly states that if a person is killed the act must be shown to be intentional on someone's part before it can be murder.

"Why should the ravings of a maniac be taken against me? On the paper she said: 'I am going down to drown.' Then at her mother's place, she undressed herself and went into the creek. This was because she thought she could walk on the water. Better bring another charge against me for attempting to murder her there.

"Did someone throw her into the water, or did she go into the water of her own accord?

"Her appeals to me to take her from the asylum were most pathetic and many nights of tears have I passed.

"Even a month's imprisonment is too much, for the only crime I am guilty of is concealing my marriage to save shame."

Hooper then began to recite a poem, but burst into tears, and sat down, having spoken three hours and five minutes.

A member of the Queen's counsel then rose and stated, "I do not intend to notice the remarks of the prisoner, but in justice to the court and to the administration of justice in this province, it is proper that I should state that a special panel of jurors was summoned to try this case. Six out of the twelve jurors selected were English-speaking and of English origin, and they and the six French-speaking jurors constituted as intelligent and unprejudiced a jury as could be found anywhere in the country.

"The jury made no recommendation for mercy. The Crown had hoped that the prisoner would accept the verdict with appropriate submission and that he would throw himself upon the mercy of the court. In that case the Crown would have urged clemency on the Court in so far as it would be proper to do so, but after the prisoner's statements and demeanor today, the Crown does not feel justified in making any request."

His Honor then addressed Hooper. "As I understood it the circumstantial evidence was so strong that it should have been the verdict. Indeed had any of your near relatives been on the jury, as honest men, they could have come to no other decision.

"You have not been tried under the French law, but under the criminal code of 1892. When you say that, you add lies to those you have told before and during this trial. There was not one word as to your race or religion during your trial. I have listened to the efforts you have just made, but I will not take time to point out all your inconsistencies; but in your present position, throwing blame on everybody, I see little to commend you to mercy. I see no grounds on which to grant your request for a new trial, but instead of condemning you to life, I will sentence you to twenty five years in the penitentiary, and John Reginald Hooper if ever a vision of Georgiana Leblanc appears to you in your dark prison life, may it persuade you to feelings of repentance for the crime."

Ironically and unlike the other stories here, Mr. Hooper probably was guilty of murder and yet did not meet the hangman.

John Hooper served 10 years of imprisonment, was released on parole and went to reside in Winnipeg. Presumably, he never did get together with the comely Alice Stapley nor sip the potent tonic labelled 'love' again.

London Swings

A county clerk at the Middlesex County Building in London, Ontario is working alone. It is late at night. There is work to be done before her holidays. Her co-workers left several hours ago. And then the elevator opens.

"Hello." she shouts, and again, "Hello." But no reply is heard.

Who could this be?

The clerk walks down the long corridor to investigate. Every few seconds she looks back over her shoulder. A chill rushes up her spine, a bead of sweat appears on her forehead, a lightbulb flickers.

"Is there anyone there?" she whispers now.

As she nears the elevator, the door closes. The elevator then moves up and stops at the third floor. A thumping can be heard on the third floor. The noise persists for some time and moves up and down the hallway. The clerk flees the building.

Who or what was that?

Some believe this activity is the work

> 1839: Hiram Lynn, Daniel Bedford, Cornelius Cunningham, Joshua Doane, Amos Pearly and Albert Clark were executed between January 7 and February 6 for their participation in the 'patriot' raid from Detroit into Windsor. The official charge against all six was 'armed invasion of the country'.

of Marion Brown, a Texas man who was hanged on May 17, 1899 for killing a London police officer. People called him Peg Leg, because he had a wooden leg and walked with a definite thumping gate. Each year on the anniversary of his death he returns; each year he startles the occupants of the building. According to lore, he swore to the officials responsible for his death that grass would never grow upon his grave.

Condemned men and woman who were hanged were often buried in the jail courtyard. This was true of Peg Leg. And he was quite right, grass never did grow on his grave. In 1981, a backhoe operator working to level the area for a parking lot discovered the body of Peg Leg. In November of 1987, Cam Johnston of the London Free Press wrote, "Orlo Miller (the local historian who wrote This Was London) was offered Peg Leg's bones for his own collection of historic memorabilia, but declined. 'I don't want the bones, but I do want them buried in a proper grave.' Peg Leg is still looking for his eternal resting place, which for the time being is in a storage room at the University of Western Ontario." His wooden leg is on display in a glass cabinet in the lobby of the Middlesex County Building!

Peg Leg is not the only soul looking for his body parts in the County Building. Cornelius Alverson Burleigh, hanged on August 19, 1830 is still looking for his head.

His story begins back in 1830 when London, set at the forks of the Thames River, was a frontier town with log and frame houses dotting a pastoral landscape. The Thames River demarcated the western and southern limits of the settlement. The population neared 300 citizens. The judicial centre of the district had been established earlier at Vittoria, southeast of London near Lake Erie. However, the courthouse and gaol were gutted by fire in 1825 and officials transferred the seat of government to London, where a new courthouse was constructed in the centre of this wilderness settlement. The original frame structure was replaced in 1830 by an imposing brick edifice. The courthouse was a replica of Malahide Castle near Dublin, Ireland, the ancestral estate of Colonel Thomas Talbot, founder of the Talbot settlement of Western Ontario. Even while it was under construction, deeds were being drawn to assure its productivity.

On the morning of September 16, 1829, Constable Pomeroy was in hot pursuit of the culprit responsible for theft, arson and destroying cattle in the area. Pomeroy was ambushed by the thief (or was it thieves?) and shot dead. One clue was found at the scene of the crime — a cap! Officials believed the cap belonged to Cornelius Burleigh, a resident of London.

A reward of one hundred pounds was posted by the District authorities for the capture of Burleigh.

In short order, Burleigh was apprehended and confined in the primitive cells of the temporary courthouse. Colonel L. A. Norton, a patriot of the Rebellion of 1837, who was also 'lodged' there, described the conditions of the jail in his book entitled, 'Life and Adventures of Col. L. A. Norton':

"While cooped up in Simcoe jail we had a large-sized sheet-iron stove in our apartment for our sixty prisoners to cook their own rations upon, and one thin blanket at night, and this in the midst of a Canadian winter. But this was comfortable when compared with our condition in the cells of the London prison. When I say the cells, of course I don't mean the cells proper. Each cell was filled, but that was scarcely a beginning, as there were over six hundred prisoners in the castle. Every hall was crowded full, and there were no blankets or other coverings save what the prisoners had on. As to the floors, they were filled with large-headed spikes, the heads sticking up about three- fourths of an inch above the floor.

Early days at the London jail.

"When the prisoners were first incarcerated at London, the guards were all raw militia and were not at all acquainted with fire-arms, and through their awkwardness several had been discharged in the prison. One gun had been discharged in the room in which I was confined, and the ball had passed directly up through the ceiling, or floor of the room above; and the contents of another piece had passed through a partition connecting two rooms occupied by prisoners.

"Prisoners were in the habit of paying the turnkeys to smuggle in liquor, the effect of which finally resulted in a disastrous row. One afternoon some of the prisoners sent out and had a twelve-quart pail full of whisky brought in instead of water, and before night some of them got pretty 'mellow'."

At the time of his arrest, Cornelius Burleigh firmly expressed his innocence of any crime. During his incarceration that winter, the other prisoners in the building made a break for freedom. Cornelius, certain of his acquittal, remained behind. As a result some citizens had doubts about his guilt. Would he not, after all, have escaped along with the other prisoners if he were guilty?

London historian and author, Orlo Miller, points out that there was wide speculation that he did commit the crime, that two Riddle brothers were probably the guilty ones.

Unfortunately for Burleigh, others did not agree that he was innocent, including the witnesses who testified against him. The jury found him guilty of murder. He was sentenced to be hanged until dead in August of 1830.

According to Miller, "Three men, two clergymen and a vacationing undergraduate, played leading roles in the last act of Cornelius Burleigh's pathetic little tragedy. The Reverend James Jackson, a Methodist circuit-rider, said to have been distantly related to Andrew Jackson, seventh president of the United States, made Cornelius his particular charge, although 'target' might have been a more accurate description of the object of his daily attendance."

The Reverend Jackson was on a dedicated mission to elicit a confession from Burleigh. After all there was no harm in it if he could gain a small amount of fame and fortune doing God's work.

According to Jackson it only took a mere forty-one hours prior to his execution to gain a dying confession. Jackson, along with Revd. Messrs. Boswell and Smith, described the ordeal stating, "Burleigh burst into a flood of tears."

In no time, the Reverend had the confession printed in handbill form to sell to the public for a modest fee of $1.50.

Burleigh, who always maintained his innocence of the crime, could neither read nor write. His written confession certainly displays the showmanship and flim-flammery surrounding a public hanging in Ontario. Burleigh's statement showed the tampering by the clergy: "I was left to wander through the world, under the influence of depravity, without the advantages of education, or religious instruction, to counterbalance the influence of my natural propensities to evil, of various kinds, particularly that of frequenting all places of profane resort. I was often found in the merry dance, and lost no opportunity of inducing thoughtless and unguarded females to leave the paths of innocence and virtue..."

In those days public hangings were a gala affair. People put their own lives on hold and travelled to London to witness the administration of the King's justice. In 1830 a London historian described the scene of the first hanging in London, "The gallows stood in the courthouse yard; almost all the people within 25 miles of London came to see the drama, and their depraved tastes were satisfied."

By Thursday, August 19, 1830, the size of the settlement of London had grown from 300 residents to 3000. Spectators travelled from nearby townships and from York, as Toronto was then called, and Hamilton to witness this public execution.

> 1867/68, London: 'Slippery Jack' ran a spree of break-ins, apparently as a bet that he could break into at least one home per week for a period of one year in London and escape arrest. He began by breaking into homes during the night to stack and rearrange furniture. The more successful he was, the braver he became until he began to shout in his victims' ears or tickle their feet as they slept. 'Jack' was prepared to repay his victims for any damages he incurred from his winnings from the bet.

Why was a public hanging so well attended?

"People were not necessarily drawn to hangings by any desire for mass vengeance. It's just that there were few entertainments available at the time," concludes Miller. And that was, indeed true. Television, movies and radio didn't exist. This was as close to live theatre as many citizens would ever see.

Jackson, Boswell, and Smith performed the religious functions at the hanging. Jackson read the dying confession from the scaffold. Mr. Smith, a Baptist minister, delivered the homily before the crowds and the closing prayer. Edward Boswell, an Anglican missionary, proceeded to baptize the 26 or 27 year-old Burleigh and to give him Holy Communion.

1868, Kingston: Thomas Jones was hanged in public on December 29, 1868, for murdering his twelve year old niece who testified against him on a charge of theft. 7,000 citizens watched Jones swing.

The spectators waited in anticipation as the hangman placed the noose around his neck. But something went wrong. The rope could not bear the condemned man's weight. As Burleigh was about to swing, the rope snapped and he dropped twenty feet to the ground, dazed but alive.

"Burleigh's conversion was complete. He walked among the crowd with the tag-end of the broken rope dangling from his neck, his whole mind devoted to prayer, prayer, prayer, praise, singing and thanksgiving." stated Miller.

Burleigh truly believed that God had saved him, but the authorities had something else in mind. Someone was ordered to fetch a new rope from Goodhue's store across the way. They were going to hang him again!

One can only imagine Burleigh's horror when he was led back up the scaffold stairway.

Miller describes what happened next, "The rope is properly adjusted and the trap sprung, to the sound of that peculiar and terrifying exhalation of breath from the crowd that seems to have been a feature of all public executions — a sound composed in part of civilized compassion, in part of savage delight."

The first act was over and some of the crowd dispersed. The majority of citizens, however, waited in eager anticipation to watch the dissection of Burleigh's body by medical professionals of the District of London and their students in the open courtyard.

By law, the court was to deliver the corpse to the surgeons who were set up there in front of the crowds. It was, after all, British tradition to perform the dissection of the body in public. Surgeons at that time could only use corpses of the condemned for teaching purposes. Herman Goodden, of *The London Free Press* described the scene in his article 'At Least 20 People Hanged in London,'"As the body of Burley began to cool, doctors, surgeons and medical professionals moved in for on-site dissection which had been promised to them by the court. Part of the crowd who had assembled for the hanging remained behind to watch this equally gruesome show as doctors and their students quite literally cut Cornelius Burleigh to pieces."

However, a special portion of the remains had already been spoken for by a man named Orson Squire Fowler. This undergraduate student from Yale University

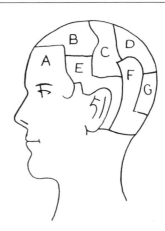

A—Area of main intellect, regarded as seat of all intellectual faculties.

B—Area related to loyalty, devotion and sympathetic qualities.

C—Area of instincts for survival and similar motivations.

D—Major control over ambitions and ability of the mind to function towards ambitious projects.

E—Here is found instincts and energy of the body and area concerned with appetite and taste buds.

F—Governs sexual side of life and also affections.

G—Deals in complex way with human being's relationship to family life and society in general.

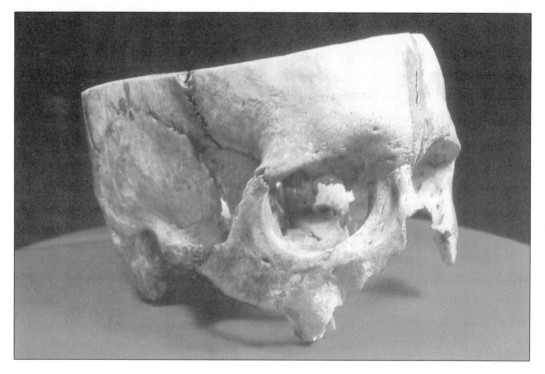

The skull of Cornelius Burleigh, on tour for 50 years and commemorated with this postcard.

had the presence of mind to obtain Burleigh's head. Fowler, it seems, was well versed in the "science" of phrenology. According to Websters Dictionary, phrenology is "the study of the shape and size of the cranium as a supposed indication of character and mental faculties".

Prior to the hanging, Burleigh had consented to see Fowler who examined his head and jotted down his findings — although it was to no avail for Burleigh.

It was not until the dissection of Burleigh's body that Fowler conducted a lecture in a dimly lit hall with the skull and a candle to illustrate the truth of his assertions. The geography of Bur-leigh's cranium bore out his predictions. Where he had said the skull walls were thin, the candlelight shone through; in other areas no light emerged.

It was Fowler's contention that the bumps on Burleigh's skull proved conclusively that he was incapable of murder, that officials had hanged the wrong man.

For the next 50 years Fowler travelled extensively using Burleigh's skull to promote his theory of phrenology as a method of criminal assessment. In the 1880's Fowler returned to London and gave Burleigh's skull to the Harris family who lived at Eldon House. Today Eldon House is a museum located down the street from the jail.

The museum kept Burleigh's skull on public display until a recent complaint caused museum officials to place it in storage in the attic. (Perhaps someone might want that skull one day!)

Occasionally, now, on moonlit nights, passersby see a shadow skirting across the parking lot of the county courthouse followed by a whisp of trailing light. This hazy form appears to dance from side to side and then stands still. A closer look reveals a human form, except for one thing, the head. There is no head. Burleigh has returned, perhaps, to find it.

When body parts are scattered, dissected or lost, when justice is not served, do those condemned return to search or seek revenge? Are they destined forever, like Ichabod Crane, to haunt paths and corridors in search of their remains? Are they never to find their resting place and truly rest in peace? Perhaps the Middlesex County Building is full of stories like these — workers there should stay on the alert for ghostly visitors.

Evil Visits the Goderich Fall Fair

The fall is a visual reminder of change, change of seasons; change of weather; change of colours and change of growth. We celebrate these many facets of change at fall fairs. On the last week of September, 1910, Goderich, Ontario was hosting its agricultural fall fair. People travelled for miles to attend the festivities, people like Elizabeth Anderson, a young woman, small of stature and delicate in appearance.

On Tuesday, September 20th at 2 o'clock in the afternoon she left her home and travelled by buggy to the fair grounds. She was smartly clad for the occasion in a white straw hat with grey and red trimmings, a short black and white plaid coat and a dark blue dress. Elizabeth had originally made arrangements with her younger brother, Willie, to meet him at the gates of the fair grounds at 9 p.m. to travel home together.

Shortly after 9 p.m. Willie stood by the gates looking about for his sister. When a few minutes passed and she had still had not arrived, Willie became concerned. He remained until nearly everyone had left the grounds and then went home to notify his parents that Elizabeth was missing.

Her father, Wesley Anderson, immediately set out in search of her. First he went uptown to the Colborne hotel, thinking that Elizabeth may have joined her older sister who was employed there. The hotel was closed and he returned home alone. At midnight he and his wife and Willie set out once more. This time he drove to the Jardine home. Young Edward Jardine was a friend of Elizabeth's and Wesley thought his daughter might be there. No one answered the knocks on the door. The family travelled next to the fairgrounds. There was still no sign of her. They went home for the night and

Wesley resumed his search with three other men at daybreak.

In the morning the search party scoured the fairgrounds and all of the buildings in the neighbourhood. Eventually they arrived at a vacant house on the west side of Eldon Street across from the south-west corner of the exhibition grounds.Wesley had searched the vicinity on the previous evening, but had not entered this boarded-up dwelling.

One of the men discovered the entrance to the cellar at the side of the building. He entered cautiously and was horrified to see a mutilated body lying on the floor. His shout brought the other men, including Wesley, who dropped to his knees and wept. The body was nude and it was the body of his little girl. Her shoes and stockings and one glove had not been removed and her hat was positioned over her face. Her other clothes were strewn about the floor.

Attached to the Goderich jail was the comfortable residence of the governor (jailer) and his family.

There was a terrible gash in her throat and her head appeared to have been battered. There was no blood on the body, but some of her clothes were drenched with blood.

Police were summoned, Crown Attorney Seager was notified and soon arrived on the grounds. A guard was stationed at the house, but not before a host of curious people, men and women, had visited the scene, seen Elizabeth's body, and tramped about in the cellar and the yard and the street. This destroyed any evidence that may have been left at the scene.

The body was removed to Brophey's undertaking rooms. The police left the clothing behind in the cellar to await the arrival of Provincial Detective William Greer of Toronto. A jury was then selected and Dr. W. J.R. Holmes acted as coroner. The jury and coroner then viewed the body. Dr. Holmes remarked that for forty-five years he had been coroner and had held numerous inquests, but he had never presided over a more heinous crime. It seemed to him to be the result of a demented mind. The jury adjourned until the following week.

On September 29th, the *Goderich Signal* newspaper summarized the events, "Since Sunday morning the town has been stirred to its depths by the discovery of one of the foulest crimes ever perpetrated in the Province of Ontario."

On Monday several clues were followed up, but without implicating anyone in the crime. Suspicion quickly fell on the foreigners living in the district. Mame Spatrao, a young Italian, had been at the fair on the same day as Elizabeth. He had spoken to the girl at 8 p.m. when he invited her to drive home with him. She had replied that she would be leaving for home at 9 o'clock. When Spatrao returned with his horse and buggy Elizabeth had disappeared. Two polish immigrants were also questioned concerning their movements. Officials were satisfied that all three suspects were in bed early and had nothing to do with the crime.

Edward Jardine, on the other hand, appeared quite agitated when questioned. He did admit to having seen Elizabeth at 7:15 p.m. on the fair grounds and said that he gave her fifteen cents to get some supper. Jardine also stated that he saw her again in the chicken

Edward Jarmine who was arrested in connection with the death of Lizzie Anderson.

house about half an hour later, standing near a man dressed in a brown suit and a fedora hat. There was a red ticket sticking out of the hat band. According to Eddie this was the last time he saw Elizabeth.

Willie Anderson now recalled that his sister had said that she was to meet Eddie at the corner at Britannia road at 9 o'clock and that he was to go home with her. Jardine denied such an arrangement. He said he and his brother Tom left the fair at 8 o'clock and returned home. The lads had been sleeping in a tent near their house. That night, however, the Jardine brothers say they found it too cold to remain out in the tent and they went back in the house after half an hour.

The clothes worn by Eddie Jardine and Spatrao on the day of the fair were examined and no blood was found.

The *Goderich Signal* reported, "Police also investigated the curious disappearance of a man named Frank Smith on the day of the murder. Smith, who was about thirty-three years of age, came to Goderich a few weeks ago to work as a varnisher in the organ factory. He went to work on the 7th and ceased work on the 15th, saying he was ill. The foreman of the factory met him on the street on Monday, the 19th, and was told by Smith that he would return to work the following day. He did not show up at the factory on Tuesday. At the boarding-house of R.A. Standish, where he resided, Smith ate his dinner on Tuesday and then left, saying he was going to the fair. He was not seen again.

He left behind a suitcase, a good suit of clothes, shirts and other articles of wearing apparel. The case contained about a dozen bottles of medicine. The effects more than offset his unpaid board bill. Smith looked and acted like a person who took morphine or some other drug and was morose and melancholy in disposition. His movements since he left Goderich have since been traced and he is out of the count in connection with the Anderson case. He was at Seaforth for several days last week."

A livery rig, a two-seated surrey, became the next focus of the investigation. Apparently on the night of Elizabeth's disappearance the rig was hired by one of the acrobatic performers at the fair. The man and a well-known resident of the town were seen driving off with two girls. The acrobat and one of the girls left the rig about midnight, while the other couple resumed their drive. The surrey was returned at 3:30 a.m. Close inspection of the rig revealed a rug clotted with blood. The authorities investigated the matter and seemed satisfied that the blood on the rug had no connection with the murder.

The inquest resumed on Tuesday. Wesley Anderson was called to testify and stated he had last seen his daughter Elizabeth about 7'clock on Tuesday morning, the 20th, at which time he left for work. He then told of his search for the girl late on Tuesday night when she had not returned from the fair grounds. He started out alone on the first trip to Goderich, but was accompanied the next time by his wife and son. They then went home and he had something to eat. He started out again at 5 o'clock sharp. He was accompanied by John Oakes, Roxy Walker and another man at 10 o'clock when they found the body.

Wesley added, "Oakes had gone down into the cellar first, and while I was at the top of the steps. Oakes turned back horrified and said, 'My God, Wes, Elizabeth is down here dead with her throat cut.'"

Crown Attorney Seager then asked, "Are you a smoker?"

Wesley answered, "Yes."

"Have you a jackknife?" asked Seager.

"Yes, do you want to see it," said Anderson.

The witness then drew out his knife and laid it on the table.

"Did you ever lend the knife to the Italian? asked Seager.

"No, never," said Anderson.

Seager added, "It was not possible for anyone but yourself to have had it that night?"

Anderson replied, "No, sir."

Detective Greer then picked up the knife and carefully examined it and handed it back to Wesley.

Mrs. Anderson was next. She substantiated her husband's testimony regarding their search for Elizabeth on the night of her disappearance. She did state that her daughter had been more or less 'intimate' with the Jardine boys. Elizabeth had been at the Jardine house on a couple of occasions.

It was not elaborated as to what Mrs. Anderson meant by the word "intimate". What was obvious was that there was a level of trust and acceptance of her daughter's relationship with the boys as she had been permitted to visit their home and to be left alone with them.

The Crown called Willie Anderson, the brother of the deceased. Willie stated that he had last seen his sister at 6:30 p.m. on Tuesday, the 20th. She was standing in the fair grounds near the fence. He had asked her when she was going home, and she had replied that she was returning home at 9 p.m. with Edward Jardine.

Not convinced of the arrangement, he had returned to the gate about 9 p.m. to make sure his sister was indeed travelling home with Edward. He waited and waited for 35 minutes before leaving the fair grounds.

Mrs. Jardine took the stand and stated that she had four sons at home: Thomas, Charles, Frank, Edward and another son, Albert, who boarded out. She confirmed that on the night in question Edward arrived home at 8 o'clock. She was sure of the time because she had looked at the clock. Thomas and Edward then left the house to sleep in the tent in the backyard. In about an hour she told the boys to come into the house as it was too cold out there. They had slept in the house that night, according to her.

She added, "On his return from the fair Edward mentioned having seen Elizabeth at 7 o'clock at the fair and given her fifteen cents. He had seen her talking to a man dressed in dark clothes and a fedora hat, with a red ticket in the band."

According to her she had not heard the Andersons when they hammered on her door in the wee hours of Wednesday morning.

The Crown Attorney then asked, "How do you account for that?"

She replied, "Well, there were some drunken men kicking up a row all night out on the road, and I could not tell one noise from another."

The Crown Attorney called Edward Jardine to take the stand.

Edward stated he had seen Elizabeth at 7:15 and had given her fifteen cents to get her supper. At another time he had seen her in the chicken coop, talking to a strange stout man. He looked at his watch when coming out of the chicken coop. It was then 7:30 p.m. He said he heard the town clock striking 8 p.m. as he was going into the gate at home. After he had entered the house he again looked at his watch and saw it was two minutes after 8 p.m.

"Your watch is very useful to you," commented the Crown Attorney.

On Tuesday evening the post-mortem examination was conducted by Drs. Gallowk, Macklin and Gunn. They found evidence that the girl had been struck a blow on the forehead, the wound being such as would be made by the knuckles of a closed fist. They believed the blow was given before the throat was cut. According to the doctors, Elizabeth was probably initially stunned from the blow and then carried in this state into the cellar, where her throat was cut with a sharp penknife. Her clothing was afterwards removed, the blood on the upper part of the garments showing in the same place in each, as if it had soaked through one garment after the other from her neck. They believed that the garments had been cut off with a knife, perhaps the same one which had been used to cut her throat.

Their theory was that the murderer or murderers, being repulsed in their attempt upon the girl, struck and stunned her and then carried her into the cellar. Fearing the consequences should the girl recover to tell the tale, they cut her throat, and possibly to hide the crime more surely, they decided to dispose of the clothes and the body in different ways and were frightened away before carrying out their plan. It had been, after all, a bright moonlit night and anyone passing near might have witnessed something.

During the inquest there was no hint or indication of sexual assault although the details of the murder would lead to conclusions of that nature.

One of the doctors informed *The Signal* newspaper, "The incision in the throat was apparently done by someone who was accustomed to pigsticking or something of that sort, as it required a good deal of dexterity to cut the throat with any but a very sharp instrument."

The townspeople of Goderich also shared their theory about the murder. Some people believed that the murderer was a local man since a stranger would not know anything about the cellar or the entrance to it. A local man would be more anxious to get the girl out of the way. Further, the girl would not likely be in that area of the town with a stranger.

The *Goderich Signal* cited this opinion, "Though rather simple-minded, she was a good girl, and would be likely to repulse advances from any person whom she did not know. The house was in the opposite direction to that which she would take to go to her home."

Elizabeth Anderson's body was removed from the undertaking rooms on Wednesday evening and taken to the home of the Andersons in Saltford. The next morning Reverend M. Turnbull conducted the funeral service at the house and her remains were conveyed to the cemetery at Dungannon.

Interest in the Anderson murder remained high. *The Signal* newspaper reported, "The inquest was resumed last night. The sitting was held upstairs in the town hall and the room was packed almost to suffocation. Evidently the Crown is endeavouring to weave a chain of evidence connecting young Edward Jardine with the sad fate of Elizabeth Anderson. Although he swore at the inquest last week that he went home at 8 o'clock, and had last seen Elizabeth Anderson a quarter of an hour before that, several witnesses were on hand who stated most positively that they saw Jardine and Miss Anderson together as late as 9:30 o'clock or a few minutes to 10 o'clock."

Mrs. Teideman was called to testify at the inquest. She stated that she did not know Edward Jardine but knew his brother Frank. She was at the exhibition Tuesday night and while in the poultry house she remembered seeing Frank Jardine and Elizabeth Anderson and another young man, of whose identity she was not certain, though she thought the first witness called (Edward Jardine) looked like him. Mrs. Teideman set the time to be about 8:30 p.m. when she saw them.

Another witness, thirteen year-old Reggie Love, reported seeing Eddie in the evening at the chicken shed. He stated a young lady was with him and he was sure it was Elizabeth Anderson. He set the time to be 8 o'clock when he saw them.

Ray Steels testified to seeing Elizabeth Anderson and Eddie Jardine standing just a little south of the grandstand. The time was 9:30 p.m.

Dr. Gallow was then called and presented his report of the post-mortem examination. "Three clots of blood below the skull above the eye would indicate that the girl had been subject to violence before death. From the appearance of the mark it was made by the knuckles of a hand. It was not sufficient to cause death but would cause unconsciousness. The fluid found at the back of the head would indicate that the blow was a severe one. The cut in the throat was the cause of death. The cut looked like the work of a knife and the stab above the large wound would indicate that it was a large jack-knife.

"The cut was made by one sweep of the knife. The blood would not squirt when it was a quick, slashing cut. The clothes were evidently on the body when the deed was done, as the upper garments were soaked with blood and the body was free from all blood marks. The skirt worn by the girl appeared as if it had been used to wipe the body."

The Crown was now intent on discovering what time the murder had taken place. Mrs. D. Buchanan stated that her home was on Eldon street, within a short distance of the place where the body was found. On the evening of the tragedy, according to her, she went to bed about 9:30 p.m. She fell asleep and was suddenly awakened by a woman's cry which was followed by men talking. There was another low cry and she heard a man laugh. Mrs. Buchanan believed the sound seemed to come from the southwest corner of the exhibition grounds.

She described the cry like a wail of distress. She testified that she was sure that she heard more than one voice. She thought the time would be about 1 o'clock Wednesday morning. Although it was a bright, moonlit night she did not look out.

Mrs. Ross lived only two houses from the scene of the crime. She also heard a cry but it appeared so close to the house that when she first awakened she thought it was one of her own children asleep in another part of the house.

"It was like a child's voice and it was a pitiful moaning cry, more of a moan than a cry," added Mrs. Ross.

She judged that the time she heard the cry was about 1:30 a.m.

A reporter for *The Signal* summarized the events to date, "The evidence so far submitted to the jury reveals nothing culpable in any person except that the Jardine "alibi" has fallen through. As late as 9:45 p.m. on the night of the murder Edward Jardine was seen with the murdered girl on the fair grounds, according to testimony given at the inquest, and the report has gained currency that a woman will testify at the inquest Friday night that she saw Jardine and Elizabeth Anderson on the night of the murder on the road leading to the house where the body was found."

Things were looking very poorly for Edward Jardine. He continued to deny the testimony of others. Even his mother attempted to resolve the situation with her account. George Tate Blackstock, K.C., of Toronto, and Crown Attorney Seager continued to question Mrs Jardine. They knew she was not giving an honest account.

Blackstock wanted to know Mrs Jardine's whereabouts prior to Edward arriving home from the fair. He began his questioning.

"Do you wish to make any alterations since your last evidence?"

Mrs. Jardine replied, "No."

Blackstock then asked Mrs. Jardine about her whereabouts on

the day of the disappearance of Elizabeth Anderson.

"I was going a piece of the way home that night with my daughter-in-law and as it struck 7 we were opposite Mr. Proudfoot's, and we met Mr. and Mrs. Teidemann."

"Where had you met Mrs. George Jardine that night?" inquired Blackstock.

"She came to my house in the afternoon about two or three o'clock and stayed till after tea," answered Mrs. Jardine.

"Then you know Mr. and Mrs. Teidemann were witnesses here?" added Blackstock.

"Yes," answered Mrs. Jardine.

"And you know they were giving some account here of having seen your son Edward, and this girl, Elizabeth Anderson, at the fair grounds," asked Blackstock.

"I saw it in the papers," said Mrs. Jardine.

"And they were endeavoring to fix the hour they saw the pair at the grounds?" said Blackstock.

Again she answered, "I saw it in the papers."

"And the change you wish to make in your evidence is that at that time you met Mr. and Mrs. Teidemann, apparently going to the show grounds, and that it was about seven o'clock?" said Blackstock.

"Yes, I heard the town clock strike," said Jardine.

"And what time did you get home? Before or after Edward?"

"Before,"

"Were you out again that night?"

"I'm sure I wasn't."

"Why are you now telling for the first time about having gone out with your daughter-in-law, having had occasion to recall all the circumstances the next day?"

"I did not think of it."

"You went out to Saltford after the murder?"

"I went over to get the mail for my son George at Saltford and called at Mrs. Anderson's."

"And it just happened one of the times was the next day after Edward had been interrogated as to this murder by Mr. Seager?"

"Yes."

"What was the conversation with Mrs. Anderson?" asked Blackstock.

"She said she thought that night while looking for Elizabeth she heard screams near the show tent, and that somebody must have carried her off." said Mrs. Jardine.

"You went to Mrs. Anderson's and said you called because you heard they were blaming your son, Edward, and she said 'Oh no, not at all', and she said, later, they had gone to the fair grounds to search and while there she was sure she heard Elizabeth screaming in a tent, and thought some show men were holding her there and that she was afraid to go near, with both her son and her husband standing near?" added Blackstock.

"Yes, the men were a short ways off," she said.

"And in spite of the screams she did not give notice to the police?"

"Yes," answered Mrs. Jardine.

"And you wish to make this addition to your former evidence. When did it occur to you?" asked Blackstock.

Jardine replied, "I thought of it immediately I gave evidence before."

"Why did you not send for Mr. Seager and tell him of this very important omission? You, of course, realize that this is an extraordinary and important statement?" said Blackstock.

"Yes," replied Jardine.

Blackstock paused for a moment, then added, "Do you know what an oath means? Madam, don't you know when you touch that book you are summoning God to witness you telling the truth"

"I'm telling the truth as nearly as I know," said Mrs. Jardine.

"Let me show you what you swore to the last time. In the first place Mr. Seager and Mr. Greer went to see you the next night after the girl was found on Monday. Then you told them Thomas and Edward slept out in the tent all night," said Blackstock.

"Yes."

"If you said then that they slept out all night, is it wrong?" asked Blackstock.

Jardine stated "It is."

"Instead of that, what do you now wish to say? They did not sleep in it till 5 o'clock. When did they first go to the tent?" asked Blackstock.

"A little after 9 o'clock, " said Mrs. Jardine.

Blackstock asked, "When did they come in again?"

"They did not stay long," added Jardine.

"Were you in bed when they went out? asked Blackstock.

"No, getting ready," responded Jardine.

"Were you in bed when they came in?" asked Blackstock.

"Yes."

"They had slept out in that tent for a long time until this Tuesday night? Blackstock asked.

"Yes," was the response.

"This was the first time they started going out, coming in and going out again in the morning in this manner?" asked Blackstock.

She nodded.

"Then some time in the night Thomas and Edward came into the house and got into that bed. You think it was 10 o'clock?" enquired Blackstock.

"Yes."

"Had your son Edward a knife?" asked Blackstock.

"I never saw him with one," she said.

"Never" said Blackstock.

"Before he got hurt. He lost it then."

"What kind of a knife? asked Blackstock.

"A blackhandled pocketknife."

Blackstock then said, "I think from all the varying stories you have told it would shake the confidence of everybody in what you are saying. It is important as you know more about this matter and are not telling us. Is it true you know no more about it?"

Jardine replied, "It is."

Mrs. Jardine was then dismissed and Mrs. Love took the stand to dispute Jardine's testimony. According to her she saw Mrs. Jardine on the street at 9 o'clock the night of the murder.

Frank Jardine took the stand later in the day and stated that he had seen his brother Edward with a black-handled knife two or three weeks before the murder; he did not know whether it belonged to Edward or not.

It was Edward Jardine's turn to be questioned by Blackstock. Edward declared that he had not discussed the matter of the inquest with his mother, brothers or anybody else and that he had not been thinking it over either. He had not had a knife since his fall at Holmes tramway in June. The knife referred to belonged to his brother Thomas, which he had, on occasion, borrowed.

A boy named Harry Irwin was called to the stand and he confronted Jardine, who was still in the witness box. Irwin said he saw Jardine about three weeks before the fair with a black-handled knife with a broken blade.

Willie Anderson, brother of the deceased, Elizabeth Anderson, swore that he saw Jardine whittling a stick with a knife a short time before the day his sister disappeared.

Blackstock asked Edward, "What do you say to that boy's story?"

Edward replied, "It's another lie."

According to Edward he did not have a knife in his possession on the day of the fair. Yet, William Fraser, an elderly man, testified that he saw Jardine at the fairgrounds on the afternoon of September 20th with a knife.

"I never saw that man in my life," replied Edward when asked by Blackstock to respond to the testimony.

George Moss, who lived a few houses from the Jardines, testified that between midnight and 2 a.m. on the night of the murder he heard what sounded like a knock at a door in the direction of the Jardine house. He thought it ought to have been loud enough to wake the Jardines; it wakened him. It was Mrs. Anderson, who had stated previously that she knocked at Jardine's door that night in her search for her daughter, but got no answer.

Blackstock then urged Edward Jardine to tell the truth. Blackstock stated, "You must realize that the evidence places you in an unfortunate position." However, Jardine protested that he was not keeping anything back.

"What is it you are thinking of this minute that you are holding back?" Blackstock shot back.

Jardine, almost with a smile upon his face, declared that he had nothing more to tell. Everyone else was lying. He was dismissed from the witness box.

Mrs. George Jardine, Edward's sister-in-law, found a black-handled pen knife on the road at the south boundary of the town, a short distance from the house in which the body was found. Could it have been Edward Jardine's knife?

On October 26, the jury of the inquest rendered its verdict, "Elizabeth Jane Anderson came to her death on the night of the 20th of September, 1910, at the town of Goderich, by her having her throat cut with a sharp knife or similar instrument, and the evidence submitted points strongly towards Edward Jardine as having committed the crime."

An hour after the verdict was read Edward Jardine was arrested and charged with the murder of Elizabeth Anderson. No newspaper accounts refer to the fate of Thomas, Edward's brother. He was charged with being an 'accessory after the fact', which meant that the authorities didn't believe he played a role in the actual murder but that he protected his brother afterward. There is also no record of his punishment.

The trial of Edward Jardine for the murder of Elizabeth Anderson commenced on April 12, 1911. The court opened with Chief Justice Sir Glenholme Falconbridge presiding. L.E. Dancey was the counsel for the prisoner.

The Signal newspaper reported, "The first witness called was Mrs. Anderson, mother of the murdered girl. Her evidence was similar to that which she gave at the inquest. She was followed by Wesley Anderson, the girl's father, and Willie Anderson, her brother, whose evidence also was along the lines of that given at the inquest."

Edward Jardine sat in the dock, chewing gum, and appeared to be disinterested in the entire proceedings.

A startling revelation occurred during the trial when Dr. Bruce Smith, Provincial Inspector of Prisons stated that during his visits to the jail over the winter, he had discovered Edward Jardine to be a "sexual pervert," although no details were ever published. Apparently, he won Jardine's confidence to such an extent that the prisoner made a confession to him. According to Smith, Jardine told of several conversations with Elizabeth Anderson on different occasions during the afternoon and evening of the murder and that he had given her money to buy a dinner. Jardine told him she was a willing party to the proposal that the deserted house be visited and in going down the cellar steps she fell and struck her head, exclaiming, 'My God, oh, I'm hurt'.

According to Dr. Smith, Jardine assisted her to the cellar. At some point a remark from the girl caused him to lose control. In his own words, 'the devil got possession of me, I took out my knife, stabbed her once in the throat, put it in again and drew it right across'.

Jardine told Dr. Smith he then cut the clothes off the girl, piled them in a heap and drew the body over towards the door. He went home and washed the knife and two or three days later while exam-

Front entrance to the Goderich jail.

ining the knife as he was sitting on the lake bank he thought he detected signs of blood on it, so he threw it over the bank and had not seen it since.

There is no record of the nature of Edward Jardine's 'sexual perversion'. Nor was there any attempt to connect that information to the original facts of the murder or to suggest his 'perversion' was a motive for the attack.

Was a "third party" confession considered to be admissible as evidence or not?

"There was a great rush for admittance to the courtroom, but as the witnesses and the men called as jurors took up a good proportion of the available space, the public had mostly to remain outside. When those attending as witnesses were excluded from the room, at the insistence of the prisoner's counsel, others were allowed to come in, and these included a considerable number of women. The women as well as the men are evidently possessed of a share of the same morbid curiosity which impelled attendance on such an occasion," read one newspaper account.

On Friday morning at 9:30 a.m. L.F. Dancey, the prisoner's counsel, addressed the jury. He spoke for three-quarters of an hour, Mr. Blackstock for one hour, and his lordship's charge to the jury occupied about three-quarters of an hour.

"There is not a title of evidence on which to base a conviction, except the prisoner's confession to Dr. Smith," Mr. Dancey declared.

Dancey continued, "Unfortunate as it is for him to traduce the character of this dead girl, I must tell you the statement this man has made. There is nothing to controvert that statement. I submit you are bound by the statement of the prisoner. There is no evidence, as my learned friend will argue, that he lured this girl over to the house, sat down with her, made indecent proposals, was perhaps refused, struck her on the forehead and dragged her into the cellar. We cannot deal with this supposition.

"There was no reason or motive for the commission of this act, the atrociousness of which is unequalled by anything we find in the criminal annals of the country. My learned friend will undoubtedly argue that there are motives, that he struck the girl before he took her into the cellar, and in a frenzy killed her to cover up his crime. But we must recall that portion of the statement where he tells of her falling on her way down the steps.

"If you come to the conclusion that there was no motive for the crime, we do not require any medical men to go into the box and tell us it was the act of a maniac, a lunatic, any person bereft of senses.

"The indictment charges malice aforethought, but where is the malice? If you find there is no malice you will be quite justified in finding him not guilty on account of insanity and to my mind that is the proper verdict in this case.

"Physicians for the defense and also Dr. Gallow, a Crown witness, gave the opinions that at the time of the crime the man, being a sexual pervert, would not have knowledge of the quality of the act.

"If this man, because of being a sexual pervert, did not know the difference between right and wrong, I submit that you cannot find him guilty of murder.

"You have undoubtedly witnessed the conduct of this prisoner as he sat in the box, the most uninterested man in the court, apparently. Our hospitals and asylums are full of such as he. Can you decide for capital punishment in his case?

"My learned friend will no doubt tell you in thundering tones that this was an atrocious crime and that vengeance must be wreaked on this man for Elizabeth Anderson's death, but you must consider that he did not understand at the time the difference between right and wrong."

It was now Blackstock's turn, "All there is in this case is the question of the legal responsibility of the prisoner. It was a convenient form of expression to say that 'the devil got possession of him. The devil had possession of him long before that. This prisoner is no lunatic, but has not as much brains as the ordinary man, just as men called in that witness box are seen to be stupid and not up to the average. He is no more lunatic than you and I. This prisoner was responsible when he told this girl to hang around the fair grounds and wait for him. He was responsible when he went with her through that hole in the fence. He was responsible when he walked with her through that wet place where she got mud on her shoes. He was responsible when he helped her over the fence at the house. He was responsible when he followed her down the cellar steps, and he was responsible when he pulled out his knife. Then, in the twinkling of an eye, it is said, he became bereft of reason, and even then was capable of looking after his own safety, though not that of his victim. There would be no law in the land if excuse were to be made for this atrocious crime.

"We are face to face today once more with the hideous lineaments of vice, its mean subterfuges, its desires to divide the responsibility of crime, and above all the whimpering of guilt for that mercy which was denied its victim. I dissent entirely from the view of my learned friend that the confession was necessary to convict the prisoner, but submit that the other evidence was sufficient for any jury to convict."

"Notwithstanding anything the prisoner had said, any jury on this evidence would be asked to convict. But the prisoner has admitted his guilt, and affected to tell the circumstances of its carrying out," stated Blackstock.

"I am sorry to hear any suggestion of improper relations between Spataro and this girl. There is absolutely no evidence, and it is against the statements of the doctors, against the conception we have formed of this little girl, and I should be sorry indeed if the stranger in our land should have this aspersion cast on his reputation. He leaves this court without any stigma on his name, and there should be no additional reproach cast on the parents of the girl.

"It is suggested that this girl went willingly with the prisoner. It may be so, but there are considerations which suggest otherwise.

"As to the blow on her head, the prisoner rather suggests that it was sustained in a fall down the cellar steps, but do you think that a fall against the steps or rubble would not have caused an abrasion? Dr. Gallow, who assisted at the post-mortem, suggests that it stunned her. It would be impossible then for her to cry out, but might she not have begun to recover from the effects? It is suggested that her throat was cut after the delivery of the blow, and indeed that is shown by the evidence of the doctors.

"What was it that really happened? Remember, gentlemen, all this talk of sexual perverts and brainstorms is mere speculation, and you must not allow it to influence you one iota farther than your judgement will carry you.

"Now the prisoner said and he can not complain if we rely on his statement — that she said something which greatly angered him before he stabbed her. As to what that is we are left in doubt, but it operated to rouse his rage and resentment. We may think that rage roused in that way was very unreasonable, but that is not the point.

"Almost within a stone's throw of this court house is evidence that would show when the prisoner went into his mother's house, what he did and what was his frame of mind. This evidence was not called. Did this prisoner procure Thomas Jardine and go back to that vacant house? Those clothes were not cut off in a frenzy, but removed with the intention of disposing of evidence of the crime. Whether he had assistance or not does not matter, except to throw light on the prisoner's frame of mind. The clothing was cut off with cold deliberation, and the intention of throwing the body down a well on the premises or disposing of it in some other way.

"Did this girl, recovering from her swoon, faintly realize what was going on, and say to him that he would have to pay for this, that she would tell what had happened?

"Now, gentlemen, sympathy in such a case as this would only get us into trouble. We have a stern duty to perform and we should greatly relax the safeguards of propriety if we hesitated to give effect to the plain evidence adduce. Gladly would I accept any other way."

So ended Blackstock's summary of the events. His Lordship's charge then addressed the jury leaving it open to them to return a verdict of murder or of acquittal on account of insanity, but intimated that one of manslaughter was out of the question. "Gentlemen of the jury," he said, " you are not to be influenced by anything you have heard or read outside this courtroom. I think I feel bound to tell you that in this case the circumstances are of that nature that there is nothing I can say that will reduce the crime to manslaughter, and that your verdict can be only one of two things: guilty of murder, as charged, or acquitted on the grounds of insanity.

"Of course it was impossible to predict in advance what line would be taken by the learned counsel for the defense. He cross-examined with great skill and great force the witnesses for the Crown, who deposed to the circumstances which it was claimed formed the chain of circumstantial evidence against the prisoner. It happens that in most cases of deliberate murder most of the evidence must be circumstantial, and unless this were the case most of the prisoners accused of murder and most of those accused of arson, would go unpunished.

"Now it is stated by the prisoner's counsel that the defense must rest upon the mental condition of the prisoner. I by no means agree with him that there was not a case even without any confessions. The case was one which never for a moment did I think of withdrawing from the jury. The prisoner was seen with this girl as late as ten minutes to ten at night. He was the last person in whose company she was ever seen alive. There is his coming, after some compulsion, to see Mr. Seager, and then his statements which are all proved to be false.

"These confessions, it was shown, were not extracted by any promise or threat, because if any officer secures a confession by telling a prisoner it would be better for him to confess, that confession is worthless. These men were far from the idea of entrapping the prisoner to confess, and in my opinion are men who are among the greatest benfactors of humanity. The prisoner was warned over and over again that they were there to investigate his mental condition. There is no doubt the prisoner at the bar inflicted these fatal wounds. It is for you to decide what his mental condition was at the time. It is no question of disease of the mind or monomania, or even a low mental type, pervert or degenerate, or whatever you like. The law has drawn a sharp line, and you will remember in all your considerations that in proving the crime the Crown is to leave no reasonable doubt. Every unlawful killing is presumed to be murder, and every man doing a crime is presumed to be sane and the onus is upon the prisoner to prove to the contrary.

"It has been reiterated throughout the case that this man is a sexual pervert. I do not know whether that is exactly applicable or not. Running all through the evidence of the doctors for the defense is the statement that any motive supplied would destroy their theory.

"Lust-passion," he continued, "is by no means what the law requires as insanity. The phrase, 'the devil got possession of me,' is frequently used. It does not indicate that there is any demoniacal influence to lead a juror to acquit a man.

"A good deal has been said about motive, or the absence of it. The learned counsel for the defense has argued strenuously that there is no such thing, and that that is a strong argument for acquittal. The learned counsel for the Crown has elaborated a theory as to what took place. Generally speaking, judges and juries cannot deal with conjecture in trying a man, but where there are facts proven beyond any doubt it is competent to read between the lines."

The Signal newspaper then reported, "The case was given to the jury at noon and the Court adjourned until 1:15. When the Court resumed at the appointed hour the jurymen were again in their places."

"Gentlemen of the jury, have you agreed upon a verdict?" Clerk McDonald asked.

"We have," several replied.

"What is it?"

There was a moment's pause, and after a deep silence throughout the room, George Andrew, of Elmville, arose, no foreman having been named, and announced:

"We found the prisoner guilty."

One reporter described the scene, "For the first time since the trial opened, the public had been admitted without restriction other than the limit of accommodation in the courtroom. There were even a couple of women in the crowd. Window sills were used as seats and every foot of standing room was occupied."

"Stand up, Jardine," ordered the clerk.

"Have you anything to say why sentence should not be passed on you for the crime you have committed?"

"No," was the reply.

"It is not my practice," said the Chief Justice in addressing the prisoner, "under these circumstances to add to the terror of the situation by dwelling upon the enormity of the crime the prisoner has committed. If you have not by this time realized the terrible nature of your offense, it is impossible that any words of mine could make you do so. In passing sentence upon you I would recommend you not to have any hope of the commutation of this sentence or its lessening to any term of imprisonment, but I would recommend you to spend the remaining days left you have on earth in preparation for the judgement of the world to come.

"The sentence of the court upon you, Edward Jardine, is that you be taken hence to the place from whence you came, and from there on Friday the 16th of June, be taken to the place of execution and there be hanged by the neck until you are dead. May God have mercy on your soul."

Jardine still didn't realize the full import of the sentence until a

The area set aside for hangings at the Goderich jail. Public tours are available.

constable escorting him back to the jail told him what the sentence meant.

A request was introduced to take the case to the Court of Appeal on the grounds that the prisoner's confession was extracted by improper means.

"I am so clear about the law that I do not think I will grant it," stated his lordship. "I might as well refuse as the Court of Appeal."

On the morning of Friday, June 16th, 1911, Reverend George E. Ross was with Edward Jardine as his spiritual advisor. According to Ross the young man showed a deep concern to meet his end in a proper spirit, engaging in earnest prayer. For half an hour he broke down, but recovered and walked to the scaffold apparently without a tremor.

The Signal wrote, "Those present at the execution, besides Ellis, the hangman from Toronto, were Sheriff Reynolds, Gaoler Griffin, Dr. Alex Taylor, gaol physician, and Mr. Ross. By order of Sheriff Reynolds all representatives of the press were excluded."

Prior to his black cap being adjusted, Jardine said good-bye to those about him, but made no further statement. At a minute or two before 8 a.m. Edward Jardine was hanged for the murder of Elizabeth Anderson. Less than sixty seconds elapsed from the time the procession started from the cell until the trap dropped. Apparently it was eight minutes and a half after the drop that his heart stopped beating.

Edward Jardine died by the hangman's noose for the most treacherous crime ever recorded in the history of Goderich-temptation gone wrong. His actions undoubtedly changed the social landscape of this picturesque community, casting a shadow on the innocence of fall fairs and romantic rendezvous for a long time to come.

Woodstock's Deadly
Tea Leaves

*E*lizabeth Tilford read tea leaves and was good enough at it to be highly recommended. Her husband Tyrrell was younger than she was; he was 31 to her almost 50. May-December marriages can be a blessing for the soul, they say, but when Tyrrell passed over on April Fools Day, 1935, it drew some considerable attention. Do you suppose Elizabeth had seen the future in their tea leaves?

Tyrrell Tilford had fallen under a spell. Ever since the night he visited Elizabeth Walker to have his tea leaves read he was a changed man. He had been seduced by an enchantress. Perhaps he should have left the tea alone! Now it was too late for that; Tyrrell was under the spell of Elizabeth; he needed her; he could no longer live without her.

Elizabeth on the other hand was no spring chicken, nor was she beautiful. She was in fact slovenly, even homely. Her passion for men had already seen two untimely deaths. The death of her first husband in England was never explained.

Her second husband, William Walker, came to Canada with Elizabeth from England in 1928. Elizabeth had worked as a nurse in England and William had been a Salvation Army officer. William took ill shortly after their arrival in Canada. Over five months he declined before he finally died of what the doctors thought had been a brain tumor. His death was not questioned at the time.

It was a fortunate circumstance for Elizabeth when she met Tyrrell, who cherished and cared for her. Tyrrell and Elizabeth Walker were married in 1931. As a wedding gift his mother, Mary Tyrrell, gave her son permission to build a modest house on the corner of her property in Woodstock. His father refused to attend the wedding. He did not approve the match nor the age difference between the bride and groom. For that matter very few of Tyrrell's relatives were invited to his home during their four years of marriage and no one really took notice of the pair until Tyrrell fell ill in March, 1935.

It was in February when Tyrrell first complained of a burning pain in his stomach while making his rounds delivering scrap metal. In March, Frank Gilchrist saw Tilford in the lane behind Sutherland's book store where he was wretching violently near his truck. The man was certainly not well.

UNDER DEATH SENTENCE
Mrs. Elizabeth Tilford, found guilty by the Supreme Court jury of the murder of her husband, Tyrell Tilford.

Elizabeth must have feared the worst, for she phoned Tyrrell's sister, Agnes Allan, and asked her and her husband, Walter, to visit them on the evening of Thursday, March 28. She said that the doctor felt Tyrrell might not live through the night and she wanted Agnes' husband, Walter, to make out Tyrrell's will. Tyrrell left everything to Elizabeth.

Miraculously alive on Friday morning, Tyrrell hastened to his parents' home. His mother answered the door. "I have come home to die. I have been poisoned," said Tyrrell.

"By whom?" inquired his mother. Tyrrell murmured, "By Elizabeth."

Mary was shocked! She could see that her son was weak. He could not walk properly but staggered, as though he were dizzy. His tongue appeared to have been slashed several times with a knife. His throat looked the same.

Dr. Lindsay of Woodstock was called immediately and upon his arrival he advised Tyrrell's mother to keep Tyrrell where he was. The doctor did not prescribe any medication.

Elizabeth Tilford, soon apprised of his whereabouts by Tyrrell's sister, Annie, was livid, "He has no business to have anything, only what I give him."

Annie replied, "He's been raving all night long. He drank a whole quart of milk and ate a dozen French pastries. I think he should go to the hospital."

"He's not going to no hospital. If he is going to die he'll die at home."shouted Elizabeth.

The next day Tyrrell rested at his parents. At about 4 o'clock he became fidgety, his nose had a bluish tinge and his hands were puffy. Early in the evening Tyrrell asked his brother, Ted, to fetch his wife. "I am going to die," he said and then he pulled his mother down to him, saying "I am going to give you one last kiss."

When Elizabeth arrived she went over to the couch and bent over him. He pushed her off and said, "Elizabeth, you've killed me. You've killed three, and you will kill no more. There is sufficient money in my insurance to bury me, Elizabeth. When I'm gone you can have your other man, Bill Blake."

Tyrrell then turned on the couch to face his family, "Mother, Dad, Ted, when I'm gone, have my stomach analyzed."

Elizabeth stood up suddenly, and with remarkable calm, under the circumstances, she said, "Well, I like that!"

She then informed the family she was staying there all night until the doctor could come on Monday morning.

Sometime around midnight, after the family had retired for bed, Elizabeth and Tyrrell left the house and returned to their home. The next day, when Ted discovered that his brother was no longer at his father's house, he went to Tyrrell's house where he found his brother in bed. Ted did not disturb his brother, who was apparently resting. It was not until the following day at 4:45 a.m. that Elizabeth called him and told him to come over right away. When Ted arrived he found him dead. Elizabeth told him that Tyrrell had wanted to live a few more hours in order to clean up the mess, meaning, in his opinion, the matter of the poison. Elizabeth insinuated that Tyrrell had come to his senses and had wanted to inform his relatives that the poisoning story was simply not true but rather part of the hallucinations that seemed to go with his illness. She said he was so remorseful of his accusations, "Before he died he had wanted a knife to cut his heart out."

An inquest was held immediately to determine the cause of death. Some family members were quite suspicious of Elizabeth. Had she, in fact, poisoned him? Tyrrell had asked his parents to have his stomach analyzed. What would the doctors find?

On April 25th, a post mortem was conducted by Dr. J.B. Poole the attending physician in Woodstock and Dr. F.S. Ruttan, medical officer of health for Woodstock. Tyrrell's heart, liver, right kidney and stomach were removed and sent to Professor Rogers, provincial analyst at the University of Toronto for analysis.

Under close inspection Professor Rogers found two grains of arsenious oxide, or white arsenic in the body of Tyrrell Tilford. He stated that the arsenic in the liver was absorbed arsenic, while that in the intestines had not yet started its way through the system. The sufficient amount of arsenic to cause death according to Professor Rogers was two to three grains.

On May 17 Tyrrell's body was exhumed for a second time. Professor Rogers and Dr. Frankish, medico-legal advisor to the attorney-general's department wanted to be sure of the initial findings and make an examination of the body at the McLevin funeral home in Woodstock. The examination of the skin showed a brown discoloration of the forehead, and a fine diffusive pink rash covering the chest. There was also a pink discoloration of the abdomen and legs, extending round the hips to the back. Rogers concluded that the pinkish discolouration of Tyrrell's skin was compatible with arsenical poisoning. He also stated that the red patch in the stomach was to be expected in the case of a man who had taken arsenic by way of the mouth.

Elizabeth Tilford was charged with the murder of her husband, the late Tyrrell Tilford. The murder trial began on September 23, 1935. C. L. Snyder of Toronto was the prosecuting counsel and C.W.

Bell, K.C. of Hamilton and Frank Regan of Toronto represented the defense. Mr. Justice Kingstone was the presiding judge.

The Woodstock Sentinel-Review recorded the court proceedings, "A few minutes after the grand jury had been dismissed to their other duties, the prisoner was brought into court by Mrs. R.G. Forbes, matron of the county jail. Mrs. Tilford was attired in a black dress, with lace collar, and did not appear to be unduly perturbed by her serious position.

"When the indictment was read to her by the registrar, Peter McDonald, she answered in a firm, calm voice: 'Not Guilty'."

Mrs. MacDougal was one of the first witnesses to testify that in 1928, prior to the death of William Walker (Mrs. Tilford's second husband), she had complained to the accused that her husband had developed an irritable temper through his illness. MacDougal said, "She told me how to prepare a dish of potatoes and carrots mixed with salts of lemon saying, 'You soon get rid of him'."

Tyrell's brother-in-law James Reid, of Mount Elgin, stated that in February of that year he had heard Mrs. Tilford discuss her husbands' accusations of infidelity, stating, 'There's bloody well got to be something done.'"

The first witness to be called by Snyder was Hutcheson Keith, druggist, who testified that on March 20th at about 12:30 p.m. a woman called him whom he took to be Elizabeth Tilford. Elizabeth had been a customer for several years and often placed her orders by phone. On the said date Mrs. Tilford asked if she could get some arsenic. She told him, "Since my husband has been collecting waste paper and garbage, the place has been overrun with rats."

Mr. Keith replied that she could indeed order arsenic. She then requested two ounces of arsenic to be delivered to her home.

Cecil Bryson, agent for the Metropolitan Life Insurance Company, was asked at the trial to reveal the details of Tyrrell's insurance policies. He said, "About a month to six weeks ago Mrs. Tilford had telephoned me asking about what equity was in the industrial policies of her husband's life.

"She said, 'Mr. Bryson, I would like to know how much money is in these policies.'

Above, a view of the Woodstock jail.
Below, area of the Woodstock jail where the hangings took place.

"I informed her the amount was $300." stated Bryson.

The next witness was Tyrrell's mother who, at age 76, was assisted to the witness box.

"At about 6:45 a.m. on Friday March 29th, he came to the house. I knew there was something very strange about that boy. He had gone down hill." said Mrs.Tyrrell, Senior.

"At 8 o'clock on Saturday evening Elizabeth came to the house. She sat down beside him and said, 'You know, honey, you should not have come here.'

"He pushed her away and said, 'You know Lizzie, that you have been poisoning me.' She said, 'Honey, you are not going to die.' Then my son said, 'Lizzie you can soon have your man with the two farms, Bill Blake.'"

His mother also repeated a story her son had told her about Bill Blake peering at him through the curtain of his bedroom on the previous Thursday night. He heard Blake then turn to Elizabeth and say, 'My God, he has had enough poison to kill 20 people."

In reference to the doctor's visit to her home on Saturday, Tyrrell's mother stated, "Tyrrell accused the doctor of poisoning him, upon which the doctor showed him what he was giving him, saying, 'You will be well by Tuesday or Wednesday.'

"Tyrrell said, 'The capsules she gives me are different. She is making them. You don't understand, I'll be dead by Tuesday.'"

The doctor advised the patient to take one tablet every four hours if the pain was unbearable, according to his mother.

Tyrell had said, "Why, she has been giving them to me every hour."

His mother also said that, in addition to being given poison in capsules, Elizabeth poured the powder on his tongue and administered it in water and in tea.

Listening intently to the statements in the dock, Mrs. Elizabeth Tilford could be seen shaking her head. At times she even took notes. It was decided by her counsel in the beginning of the trial to not place her on the stand for questioning.

Mrs. Agnes Allan, a sister of Tyrrell's, said she had seen Elizabeth come from Tyrrell's room with a capsule in her hand, saying, "I have just given Tyrrell a capsule, and he has brought it back up. The doctor says he is to have one every hour."

Mrs Allan said, "Then she broke the capsule and threw it into the stove."

Eyebrows were raised concerning the next statement by Agnes Allan. "On the night of the funeral she had her husband out of the coffin. I heard her say, 'Yes, Alice, I've had him out of the casket, and turned him over. I saw he had his underwear on. I had my other husband out of the casket, too. They are not going to put anything over on me.'"

James W. Tilford, the 75-year-old father of Tyrrell, had not been present at his son's wedding. At the time he had said, "A man of 31 marrying a woman of 50 was reason enough not to attend."

When James took the stand he informed the jury of the events on the Friday before his son's death, "He sort of came bumbling in head first. He was black as a sweep. I'll bet his hands hadn't been washed for a week."

On the Saturday night when Elizabeth visited the house she said that Tyrell would soon get well. His father replied, "You bloody great cow."

Frank Tilford, another brother, stated that the last time he had seen his brother his physical condition had appeared to be normal. After his brother's death he came to Woodstock, arriving on the evening before the funeral.

"I said to Lizzie that this was kind of sudden, and she said: 'I have seen him failing for quite a while.' I went back in the evening and Lizzie said 'Your father has been accusing me of poisoning Tyrrell, and if he goes any further with it I will have every cent he had got. If your dad is going to have this boy's stomach out, and if he does, it will cost him $3,000 and a public apology in every newspaper in Canada.'"

He further testified that Mrs. Tilford gave him two capsules and asked him to take them to Toronto to have them analyzed. Frank told her that he was not fool enough to think that she would give him the capsules if she had poisoned anybody and he refused to take them.

"Did you have any further conversation with Elizabeth Tilford?" asked Crown Attorney Snyder.

"Yes, my brother Tom and myself made a third visit."

At one point Elizabeth had said she had bought poison just to kill the rats living around the house.

The Tyrrell brothers intended to find out the truth about that poison being used for killing rats. They decided to lay a trap and they went over to visit Elizabeth.

Tom said, "Lizzie, a great big rat ran across my feet outside, as I was coming in." She said, "Oh, Tom, there are no rats around here since we have been here."

Frank also related a strange remark that had been made by Elizabeth. "It will not be long until I will talk to Tyrrell," Frank asked her what she meant. She replied, "I can see you don't believe in spiritualism."

Mr. Snyder questioned yet another brother, William E. Tilford of Woodstock. On the Saturday before Tyrrell's death, William and his wife went to his father's house to see his brother. "Tyrrell," William said, "looked a very sick man." Tyrrell was suffering from repeated attacks of vomiting — five in all, while William was present. His brother's face was sallow, and his tongue was a dirty orange-brown colour, bordering on the colour of copper.

After one particularly violent vomiting spell, William suggested that Tyrrell might be suffering from gas and suggested bicarbonate of soda might give some relief. Tyrrell replied, "It's no use, Bill, my wife has been giving me poison."

According to William, his wife responded, "Can you imagine him making a statement like that, accusing his wife of giving him poison?" William attempted to tell his brother his accusation might be unjust. Tyrrell said, "It is the truth, Bill."

C.W. Bell, K.C., then began his cross-examination of Dr. Frankish. Mr. Bell elicited the fact that no post-mortem examination was made when the body was first exhumed on April 25, at which time the heart, liver, right kidney and stomach were removed, and compelled Dr. Frankish to admit that in making his autopsy at the time of the second exhumation on May 17 he had not been able to examine these organs. Therefore, he could not swear that the deceased had not died as a result of a diseased condition of one of them.

A *Woodstock Sentinel-Review* reporter added, "Referring to the famous Armstrong poison case in England (a woman's body had been preserved intact for a ten month period and traces of arsenic were still discovered), Mr. Bell suggested that Mrs. Tilford, who had been a nurse in England, and therefore knew something of the preservative properties of arsenic, was hardly likely, if she had had homicidal intentions in her mind, to have built up evidence against herself by the use of this poison. Dr. Frankish agreed that this was so, but declared that while a nurse would know of the poisonous quality of arsenic, he did not believe she would know anything about its preservative effect, for on this point even medical men were not in agreement."

Mr. Snyder asked, "Supposing you leave arsenic out of the question, was there anything in the condition of that body, to indicate the cause of death?"

"No." replied Dr. Frankish.

"But, knowing that Professor Rogers had found two grains of arsenic in the body, would you have any difficulty in certifying the cause of death?" asked Snyder.

"None whatever." answered the doctor.

Snyder continued, "And what would you certify?"

"Arsenical poisoning." stated Frankish.

Going on to speak of the cumulative effect of arsenic, Mr. Snyder asked if death might be expected to result from a fatal dose taken after three days rest, if smaller and non-fatal doses had been administered for a week or ten days previously. Dr. Frankish answered in the affirmative, but, on the other hand, stated in reply to the judge that persons had been known to survive a fatal dose of arsenic for ten days or so, and then die without any further dose.

Mr. Bell then suggested that in this case the arsenic was either administered homicidally in small doses, or suicidally in the same way, to which the witness agreed.

"Would you expect that a woman whom we are told was a nurse in England would know of the properties of arsenic?" Mr. Bell asked.

"I think she would, as a poison." answered the doctor.

Proceeding, Mr. Bell suggested that in order to state definitely the cause of death, even when an irritant was present, it was necessary to eliminate all other possible causes of death, and that this could be done only by an examination of three great cavities of the body, the head, chest and abdomen. The witness agreed.

"But through no fault of your own, you had no opportunity to examine the heart," Mr. Bell went on, "and you cannot swear that there was no disease of the heart that might have killed Tyrrell Tilford?" stated Bell.

"No, I cannot." answered the doctor.

"And you never got a chance to examine the liver?" Bell asked.

"I did not." said Dr. Frankish.

Bell then asked Dr. Frankish if he ever examined the gall-bladder. The doctor had not seen it. This led Bell to point out that Dr. Frankish had no chance to form an opinion on the gall-bladder as far as jaundice was concerned. Nor did the doctor examine the right kidney.

Dr. Frankish admitted, too, that since the stomach, possibly containing poison, had been placed in the same receptacle as the other organs, it could not definitely be said that the poison from the stomach had not impregnated the other organs.

The doctor admitted that Dr. Poole, in removing the various organs, had left the cut ends of the oesophagus and the duodenum open, as well as various arteries, veins and ducts, but he denied that there was an advanced state of putrefaction, when he made his autopsy three weeks later.

To the suggestion that it would be impossible, in view of all these openings, to say just what amount of arsenic was contained by any one organ, the doctor stated that since the stomach was ligatured it would be possible to determine the exact amount in it, but that there might have been a seepage from the open intestines on to the other organs.

Quoting from a text-book, Mr. Bell drew attention to the fact that a strangulated hernia or an intestinal obstruction might cause symptoms similar to those of poisoning. Dr. Frankish agreed that this was so, but pointed out that his examination of the intestines excluded both of these possibilities.

"You know that this man was to have an operation for a hernia?" asked counsel.

"I did not know that, but my examination showed that he did not die from strangulated hernia." declared the doctor.

For the first time in her three day trial Elizabeth Tilford began to show the strain she was undergoing. In the afternoon she began to weep in the dock and was on the point of fainting when she was assisted from the courtroom by the matron. She returned in a short time, somewhat composed.

Mr. Bell also cross-examined Dr. Lindsay, who at the time of Tyrrell's death had written the death certificate claiming the cause of death as myo-carditis, with catarrhal jaundice and influenza. He made his line of defense very clear when he said, "I am going to very seriously dispute the fact that death ever occurred from arsenic poisoning." He then began to embark upon a technical discussion of the symptoms of the three diseases listed on the death certificate with Dr. Lindsay.

"One of the most violent types of influenza is the gastro-intestinal type, is it not?" asked Mr. Bell.

"Yes." Dr. Lindsay admitted.

"And gastro-intestinal influenza, quite apart from the presence of arsenic, frequently causes death?"

"Yes." answered Dr. Lindsay.

"And Tilford had, from your observation, five of the symptoms of influenza—nausea, vomiting, abdominal pain, collapse and jaundice?"

"Yes." said Dr. Lindsay.

The last witness was William Percy Blake, a 42 year-old widower residing on a farm near Woodstock, who, according to the evidence of several members of the Tilford family, was regarded by Tyrrell Tilford as his rival for the affections of his wife, Elizabeth.

The Daily Sentinel-Review reported, "Blake stoutly denied having used terms of endearment to Mrs. Tiford in her home on the day of the funeral of her husband, as at least two of the deceased's brothers had testified and told an interesting story of how he had long been interested in tea cup reading and had first made the acquaintance of Mrs. Tilford two years before when he was directed to her home by friends to have his tea leaves read.

"Telling of more recent visits to the home he denied being there Thursday night preceding Tyrrell Tilford's death. His last visit to the Tilford home prior to Tilford's death on April 1, he said, was on March 17, when he was one of a party invited to celebrate a birthday."

On Wednesday, October 2, the fate of Mrs. Elizabeth Tilford, charged with the murder of her husband, was placed in the hands of the jury at 2:30 p.m. Judge Kingstone first explained various points of law, and the duty of the jury in such cases.

"There is this to be considered," said his lordship. "Do you think it likely or reasonable that this man had any reason for taking poison himself? What would he poison himself for? Why should he commit suicide? What motive had she in administering poison to him — because in a case of this kind, as in every murder case, one naturally looks for motive. It is suggested there was a motive. There was this question about the insurance. She went to see the insurance agent some weeks before he died and found out there was some $300 coming on his death. Then there is the other suggestion that she would be a widow again and draw a widow's pension. There is the third suggestion that she, under the will, would get this little property, whatever it was worth, and finally there is the suggestion that she would be free to marry or form an alliance with this man Blake if the husband was out of the way."

Referring to the evidence that Mrs. Allan had given "taking her husband out of the casket," the judge asked, "What do you think of a woman who would do that, gentlemen? I think it is extraordinary behavior, to put it mildly. Was it for the purpose of satisfying herself whether some authority had been making an investigation? It may have been of no significance, gentlemen, but you have got to consider it."

"You have all these facts to consider," his Lordship concluded, "and one thing you have to consider is whether Tilford's statements were made in his right mind, knowing what he was saying and under no delusion or hallucination."

Mr. Snyder opened his address by stating, "This is one of those rarely beautiful Canadian October days, but there is one person who is not able to enjoy it. A great deal has been said about the poor accused, but not so much about the poor man who lies in his grave, mutilated and cut to pieces in an effort to determine the manner of death.

"It might be said that the marriage between this young man and a woman 15 years his senior was a mistake. Did she want to get rid of him? It has been said that Tilford was complaining in February of a burning pain in his stomach, but it was at this time that the accused had been making enquiries as to the amount of his insurance. Was it likely that this man, had he been committing suicide, would have gone to his mother and sought her advice?

"Dr. Frankish, who had examined thousands of bodies, has sworn that arsenic was the cause of Tyrrell Tilford's death, and, even after Mr. Bell's cross-examination, he has repeated that he had no hesitation in saying that death had been due to this cause.

"Who are you going to believe?" He asked. "A doctor or a lawyer?"

Mr. Bell began his summation, "Why did Tyrell not try to get away from this woman who, he said, was giving him poison. The answer is this - there was arsenic in his body, not enough to cause his death, it is true, but it was there, because he took it himself. Why was he able to say, 'I'll be dead by Tuesday' when he died on the Monday. Why was he able to state the time? How did he know that he was being given arsenic, a colorless, tasteless poison, if it were not for the fact that he had it in his possession himself?"

Dealing with the subject of motive, Mr. Bell asked if the accused were likely to get rid of her husband for a sum of $300 in insurance, or $175 after the funeral expenses had been paid? Was the motive her "man with the two farms," Blake? After seeing the man Blake in the box, he asked, were the jury going to believe that. Blake, he said, had gone to the house with one of the Tyrrell boys, whose age was not far from his own, for a tea cup reading, for which he paid. On hearing of the death, he had gone to the house, wishing to help the family as much as he could.

"And when Elizabeth lay across the coffin and cried 'Honey, why have you left me to face it out alone,' was that the act of a murderess?" he asked. "No, a thousand times no."

Mr. Bell, according to The Sentinel-Review, "reminded the jury that before proving that death had been the result of arsenical poisoning, the crown had first to prove that all other possibilities of death had been excluded. Dr. Frankish, he said, had readily agreed with this proposition, but, Dr. Frankish had also admitted that the heart, which another doctor had said was affected by a disease known as myocarditis, had been taken away. Dr. Frankish had also agreed that he had not been able to see the liver, heart or stomach either."

"How can a pathologist say that he has excluded all other possibilities of death when he admits that four of the organs were never seen by him?" asked Bell.

Explaining his reason for not putting Mrs. Tilford in the witness-box Mr. Bell said, "The responsibility was entirely mine. I would not dare to put her through this morass of suspicion and wild accusation."

"I end this case as I began." he concluded. "I told you then that this woman is entitled to rely on the protection that the law affords her. I am sure you will have courage to meet and dispose of your task."

At 8:40 p.m. the jury returned to the courtroom after six hours of deliberation. The Woodstock newspaper wrote, "Sentence of death was pronounced by Mr. Justice Kingstone. The prisoner, who had gasped out a loud 'Oh' as the jury's verdict was announced, called out even before the judge had finished the dread sentence: 'Oh, your lordship, it's not right, it's not fair. Oh, if I could only have a chance to give my evidence. Oh, your lordship, I have been framed, absolutely framed. God have mercy on the Tilfords' souls.'"

After the verdict Judge Kingstone addressed the jury. "I am sure the responsibility of this very important case has weighed very heavily upon you." he said. "Let me say that I am proud of the jury, for I know what it costs a jury to bring in a verdict of this kind. The county of Oxford is to be congratulated in having a jury sitting on this case with the courage to bring in a verdict of guilty.

"I think I can say that I concur with the verdict." his lordship added.

"The sentence of the court on you, Elizabeth Tilford, for the crime of which you have been found guilty, is that you be taken from the place where you now are to the place whence you came and there be kept in fullest custody, until the seventeenth day of December, and be taken forth to the place of execution, and there be hanged by the neck until you are dead. And may God have mercy on your soul,"

The fourth murderer to go to the scaffold in Oxford county, Elizabeth Tilford awaited the final hour. Shortly before midnight on December 17, Elizabeth was observed to be almost in a fainting condition in the corridor outside her cell, but was revived by one of the matrons, who fanned her with a newspaper. A dozen reporters began to congregate round the jail wall. According to the Sentinel-Review, "It was at 12:50 p.m. that final preparations were made for the execution, when three provincial police officers entered the southeast jail yard through a doorway over which a light had been installed.

"The scaffold, stated to have been erected by Robert S. Barnett under the direction of Sam Edwards, public executioner for Ontario, had been tested previously by dropping a bag of sand of approximately the same weight as the condemned woman. The double trap-doors, heavily weighted, worked perfectly when the lever released the well-oiled bolts, and the noose had been placed in position."

At 12:59 a.m. a small procession appeared in the doorway leading into the jail yard. Elizabeth Tilford, dressed in black and without a hat, was in the centre of it, with a guard on either side. A newspaperman reported the last minutes of her life. "Elizabeth walked steadily, with her head slightly bent and her face a deathly white. The walk from the door to the death-house was a short one of about twenty paces or so, and her step never faltered, although, as was learned later, she had not required the subcutaneous injection of morphine which is frequently given to condemned prisoners before their execution.

"With her walked Mr. Dixon, who recited a passage from Scripture as the party made their way to the thirteen steps leading to the gallows. The minister stayed with her until the end, repeating a prayer while the hangman swiftly pinioned the condemned woman's limbs, placed the black cap over her head, adjusted the knot, and released the trap doors."

The execution took place in a space of only 45 seconds from the time Mrs. Tilford entered the yard until she dropped from sight into the merciful obscurity of the tarpaulin which shrouded the lower part of the scaffold. She remained on the platform for a period of little more than ten seconds.

Office where death cell once was in the Woodstock jail.

There was no sound from the time Elizabeth entered the yard until there was the thud of the opening trap. A scream or a shriek of laughter was heard from a woman outside the jail wall. Several automobiles drove up and down the street by the jail, honking their horns.

The body was then taken down. Elizabeth's children claimed the remains and a funeral service was held that morning at 2:30 a.m. The burial was performed by Reverend Stanley Dixon. It was a ghostly sermon with the reverend holding a flashlight, while he read his written words. "This soul has returned to the Lord from whence it came," said Mr. Dixon. "In the midst of life, we are in death. We here commit her body to the grave."

Elizabeth's family did not attend the funeral; the grave was unmarked; her body was placed at the corner of her second husband's grave.

Doug M. Symons in his book entitled 'The Village that Straddled a Swamp,' wrote,"Despite Lizzie's claims of innocence, the rest of the arsenic she claimed not to know about was found in the original Keith's Drug Store package, wrapped in oil cloth in a jar of mustard pickles."

Perhaps Elizabeth neglected to read her tea leaves. They may have informed her that a May-December wedding was no blessing at all but, in their case, a curse.

The Ballad of a Murderer

"I was running to Buffalo
To make my escape
When the Chief of police at Niagara Falls
Nabbed me in my race.
He landed me in Woodstock jail
Where I was condemned to die,
On the 14th of November, 1890
Upon the gallows high.
Three cheers for lawyer McKay
Who did so much for me.
Likewise to lawyer Blackstock
Who tried to set me free.
Sir John Thompson would not pardon me
I'll tell you the reason why.
Because he thinks I'm guilty
And this day I am to die."

J.R. BIRCHALL

This ballad was penned by some anonymous minstrel, commemorating the hanging of John Reginald Birchall.

In February of 1890, Inspector John Wilson Murray of Toronto carefully felt his way through the dense underbrush, the quicksand bogs and the sinkholes of the Blenheim swamp in Oxford County, Ontario. Local lore attributed "lurking evil" and witchcraft to the eerie energy of this mile and a half stretch of wilderness.

JOHN REGINALD BIRCHALL

Murray was unconcerned with folklore; he was determined to discover a body—a body rumoured to be in a small clearing here. No tales of disappearing travellers would stop him, not even the knowledge that the swamp was too soft at this time of year could sway his determination.

On Friday, February 21st, Joseph and George Eldridge ventured to the fringes of the swamp to gather firewood. They all feared the place, but they were in need of the wood. Joseph stayed to the edge, no dread swamp trails for him! George, on the other hand, proceeded cautiously into the interior. He came unexpectedly into a tiny clearing where he stumbled and fell face first. He rose to his feet and hesitantly turned to see what had tripped him. There lay the body of a man, frozen stiff. One foot was propped up on the stump of a tree. It was a hideous sight. His clothing had been partially pulled back, exposing his naked chest. George shouted to his brother and scrambled home to report his grisly discovery to the local constable. Wood was forgotten for the time being.

Inspector Murray was taken to the site. He studied the corpse for a moment and then propped the body up against the stump. Next he stepped back, sat down across from the victim, took a moment to ponder the scene and gazed into the face of death.

"I looked at it as if it were a man asleep. He was little more than a big boy, a gentle lad, a youth just out of his teens, a refined son of refined parents," said Murray.

The murder victim was a clean-shaven youth dressed in a brown tweed coat and vest, black pants with grey stripes, a brown felt hat and clean linen shirt. Murray asked his silent study, "Who are you?" It lurched forward and fell on its face.

In the back of his head was the purplish black hole made by a .32 calibre bullet, and near the nape of the neck was another. He had been shot from behind; perhaps he never knew who shot him.

His clothing was English in style and cut, with a checkered, caped mackintosh. The underclothing was also of English make; Inspector Murray had ordered some of the exact-same kind only months before. There were no apparent clues to his identity. The name of his tailor and the label on his clothes had been carefully cut out. The label in his brown Derby hat had been removed. Murray noticed that even a (possibly) tell-tale button had been severed.

The inspector then crawled over the surrounding ground, and found a crimson trail. He followed it back a few paces, and it stopped in a blotch of blood. "It was here the murder had been done, here the shot had been fired, here the victim had fallen."

The body was photographed and copies circulated to newspapers in Canada, the United States and England. Murray trusted that someone somewhere in the world would recognize the photo and he would know the identity of this corpse!

On three separate occasions he returned to the murder scene, convinced he would discover some clue. His diligence was rewarded when a cigar-holder with an amber mouth-piece marked 'F.C.B.' surfaced. It was half buried, as though stomped on.

The crime scene, Detective Murray is second from the left.

An autopsy revealed that the young man had been dead a few days but not more than a week.

Five days passed and still no one identified the body. By now it had been buried at Princeton, a town situated a few miles from Blenheim Swamp.

It was on the sixth day that a dapper young man and a woman arrived in Princeton and asked to see the body. The couple had recently crossed from England on the same ship as a man who resembled the picture in the papers. The officials exhumed the body for possible identification.

Fred Benwell

The couple stared in disbelief; was their fellow passenger. They were horrified and amazed.

"His name, we think, was Benwell," they said. "He was merely a casual acquaintance aboard ship, and we knew nothing of him."

The couple went from there to Paris, about ten miles from Princeton.

Inspector Murray was notified of the identification and set out immediately for Paris. He interviewed them in the upstairs parlour of their Paris hotel.

His trained gaze observed the young couple. He later described them, "The gentleman was dressed in perfect taste. He was handsome and easy in manner, with a certain grace of bearing that was quite attractive. He came toward me and I saw that he was about five feet, nine inches tall, supple, clean cut, well built. His hair was dark and fashionably worn; his forehead was broad and low. He sported a light moustache. Clearly he was a man of the world, a gentleman, accustomed to the good things of life, a likeable chap, who had lived well and seen much and enjoyed it in his less than thirty years on earth. The lady stood by the window looking out. She was a slender, pleasant-faced blonde, a bit weary about the eyes, but evidently a woman of refinement."

"You knew the young man?"

"Yes, very slightly," replied the stranger.

"I am glad to hear it," Murray said. "At last we may learn who he is. Where did you meet him?"

"In London."

"London, Ontario, or London, England?"

"He came from London, England. He was a mere casual acquaintance. I met him, don't you know, on the ship."

"His name?"

"I think it was Bentwell or Benswell or Benwell. I knew him very slightly."

"What ship?" Inspector Murray asked.

"The Britannic of the White Star Line. We arrived in New York on Friday, February 14."

"When did you last see the young man alive?"

"He was on his way to London, Ontario, and, as we were travelling to the Falls, our way was the same. I last saw him at the Falls. He had a great deal of luggage there. He left some of it, in fact."

"I'm very glad to know this," Murray said. "You'll be able to point out his luggage?"

"Yes. I'll be glad to help you. We're returning to the Falls today. We came here because we saw the picture in the paper."

"Your name, sir, so that I may find you at the Falls?"

"Birchall. Reginald Birchall of London —London, England."

The inspector was paying particular attention to Birchall's off-hand manner. As for Mrs. Birchall she constantly paced up and down the room. She definitely showed signs of being nervous. Murray wanted to find out more about this couple.

"How was the young man dressed when you last saw him"? asked Murray.

Mr. Birchall placed his hand on the sleeve of the Inspectors navy blue overcoat. There was no tremor in Birchall's hand. "Like that," Birchall stated.

The Birchalls at Niagara Falls.

"A whole suit of that colour?"

"Yes."

"Would he take a glass, do you know?" asked Murray.

"Oh, yes, he used to get very jolly."

The inspector then reached into his pocket and produced a notebook. Looking Mr. Birchall straight in the eyes he stated, "I am greatly indebted to you, my dear sir, for your kindness. This information is most valuable. It tells us just what we wish to know. May I trouble you to repeat it, so that I may note it accurately?"

Birchall nodded.

They continued a few more minutes.

"I bade him goodbye at the Falls," Birchall concluded, "and he went on to London, Ontario."

"Have you heard from him since?" inquired Murray.

"Just a line," Birchall stated.

"Have you got it?"

"Have I got Fred's note, my dear?" Birchall asked his wife.

"No," she replied, "but I remember seeing it."

"It was just a note to get his luggage through," added Birchall.

"His first name was Fred?" Inspector Murray asked.

"I think so," Birchall answered,. "It was so signed in the note."

The interview ended and the Birchalls left for Niagara Falls. Inspector Murray was suspicious. He immediately telegraphed the police at Niagara Falls, and asked them to shadow Birchall but not to arrest him unless he were to attempt to cross into the United States.

Murray soon discovered that the dead man was Fred C. Benwell, son of Colonel Benwell, a retired army officer, of Cheltenham, Gloucestershire, England. Furthermore, he learned that Birchall and his wife had arrived from England in Woodstock, Ontario in the autumn of 1888. However, his name was not Birchall then. He was known as Lord Somerset, Frederick A. Somerset. His wife was Lady Somerset. They became familiar figures around the countryside. They not only lived gaily, but dressed loudly and seemed to have money. His eloquence and charm enchanted the gentry. He was a handsome and charismatic man who seemed to cast spells upon the people he met. He played his chosen role of 'Lord' extremely well. The 24-year-old charmer often went driving with his wife and they frequently shared picnics about eight miles from Woodstock near Pine Pond, by the Blenheim Swamp. According to the locals, Lord and Lady Somerset had been suddenly called away. They left numerous unpaid bills.

That was it for Murray. He immediately wired Scotland Yard to request any available information about Birchall before he came to Niagara Falls.

In Niagara Falls Detective Murray found out that the murdered man, the Birchalls, and another young Englishman, Douglas Raymond Pelly, had been residing at the Baldwin Hotel. Murray interviewed Pelly, hoping to shed some light on the case. His gut instinct was right. Douglas Pelly was more than willing to tell his extraordinary story.

Pelly had just completed his studies at Oxford and was looking for adventure. The English papers often ran stories and advertisements declaring the virtues of Canada as a land of opportunity for men with some capital. In early December of 1889, an advertisement caught his eye. It read:

> "Canada. University man, having farm, wishes to meet gentleman's son to live with him and learn the business with a view to partnership; must invest 500 pounds to extend stock. In today's money, 500 pounds is worth $12,500. Board, lodging, and five per cent interest until partnership arranged. Address J.R. Burchett, Primrose Club, 4 Park Place, St James, London."

In short order Douglas Pelly responded to J.R. Burchett and received a reply on December 9, from J.R. Birchell. The different spelling was intentional, since Birchall at the time was haunted by creditors. On December 13, Birchall met with Pelly and his father. He enthralled them with a description of his Canadian property. He told them his farm was located a mile and a half from Niagara Falls, Ontario. There were large brick houses heated by steam and lighted by gas and there were many outbuildings. The farming business was large and profitable and involved the purchase of horses to be groomed for sale. He also told them that several hired men worked the farm and there was a branch business located at Woodstock where he and Mrs. Birchall often resided.

The Pellys were won over and by January 11, 1890, Birchall had a letter from Douglas and an advance cheque for one hundred and seventy pounds; he hoped to meet him at the beginning of February.

On February 5 Douglas met Mr. and Mrs. Birchall in Liverpool and boarded the Britannic, bound for New York. Pelly was immediately introduced to a fourth member of the party, Fred C. Benwell. Pelly was surprised to see him and wanted to know why Benwell was part of the group. Birchall replied that Benwell was simply travelling to another farm near his property.

The travellers all arrived in New York on February 14 where they stayed at the Metropolitan Hotel. The following day they set out on the two-day journey to Buffalo. The morning after their arrival in Buffalo Reginald Birchall and Fred Benwell left at 6 p.m. on a train bound for the farm in Woodstock. Benwell was to remain there and Burchall was to return to escort Mrs. Birchall and Pelly to the estate.

That same evening, at 8:30 p.m., Reginald Birchall returned alone. His shoes and trousers were muddy. He told Pelly that he had taken Benwell to the farm, but that he had refused to remain there. Birchall said he then gave Benwell a list of friends in the area where he might be able stay. Birchall evaded any more questions by complaining of fatigue and retired to bed. The next day they crossed the border and settled in at Mrs. Baldwin's house in Niagara Falls on the Canadian side.

Douglas Pelly continued his story. "Soon after our arrival, Birchall invited me to go for a walk. I went. We walked along the river road which goes from the village up to the Falls. I had told him about ten minutes before that he was failing to fulfil the representations he had made to me. He had replied with a shuffling explanation, and I mentally decided to give him another week, and if matters did not change, I would leave him.

"On our walk we came to a place where Birchall said a religious body in past years had held camp meetings, and it was thought it would be nice to bathe in the river, so a stairway was built down over the cliffs with the idea that they could go down it to bathe, but it had been found impossible to bathe there because the current was too strong. Birchall said to me: 'Oh, you have never been down here. You ought to go. It is the best way to see the Falls.'

"I told him I should like to go down, and he stepped aside for me. I went down first and soon noticed it was a rotten, unsafe stairway. It led down close by the Falls. 'Birchall,' I said, 'This is a horrid place.'

'Go on, it will pay you,' he said."

His recounting was a suspenseful one. They did, indeed, go down those rotten stairs that wound to the escarpment. Luckily another brave soul also ventured the trek or Pelly may not have made the return flight. He would never know. Birchall was rendered moody and silent for the balance of that day. There would, no doubt, be another day!

Well there was —the very next day, in fact. This time it was to the cantilever bridge. Underneath this bridge one could not be seen, between the brickwork of the span and the edge. Birchall took Pelly there, ostensibly, for a better view of the rapids and there he coaxed him to 'stand close to him at the edge'. Fortunately for Pelly, Birchell's cold, silent, suspicious manner caused Pelly to instinctively draw back.

When they returned to their rooms they found a newspaper article which told of a murder near Woodstock. The following morning Birchall suggested that Pelly should go to Woodstock to see if it was Benwell. As his suspicion and alarm were mounting, Pelly armed himself with a pocket revolver.

Concerned now for Benwell, Pelly accompanied Birchall to the American side of the border to check on his supposed 'luggage'. Once there, Birchall expressed a desire to stay on the New York side but Pelly protested because Mrs. Birchall was waiting at the Baldwin Boarding House.

This time they headed back on foot across the lower suspension bridge during a winter storm. Birchall again attempted to lure Pelly to the edge to view the rapids with 'a superb view'. When Pelly refused Birchall became more menacing until it was a fairly confrontational setting. Once again Pelly was saved by other travellers on foot.

Pelly was getting nervous; Birchall was nearing desperation.

The next day Birchall went to Buffalo to see about some message he said was from Benwell. When he returned he said Benwell had sent a message to forward all his heavy luggage to the Fifth Avenue Hotel in New York. The very next day a picture of the dead man was circulated in the paper.

"That looks like Benwell," Pelly declared to Birchall.

Birchall replied that it was impossible, as Benwell was to be in New York. At that juncture, Pelly offered to go to New York to see if Benwell was at the Fifth Avenue Hotel and the Birchall's went to view the body. There was no trace, of course, of Benwell in New York.

Pelly was convinced that Birchall was a shady character, possibly capable of murder.

Detective Murray was a shrewd and skillful investigator. He was not ready to apprehend Birchall yet. He had only Pelly's story. No witnesses had come forth to place Birchall at the scene of the crime. He decided to wait Birchall out, to watch for his next move. Meanwhile, he continued to build his case.

Scotland Yard responded to his request for information about Birchall. John Reginald Birchall had been born in the village of Church Kirk, Lancashire, England in 1866, the youngest son of the Reverend Joseph Birchall, the village vicar. Young Reginald received a strict religious and classical education. His father had been a scholar at Oxford, and tutored his son in English, Greek and Latin. The father placed his son in Rossall, one of the famous public schools of Britain. There he excelled in science and in sports.

After his father's death Reginald was removed to another school and had begun to display the ways of a loafer. He enjoyed most of his time in tavern parlors cohorting with individuals of low character. It was on his second attempt to qualify for entrance into Oxford University that he began his studies as a gentleman commoner of Lincoln College. He

John Robert Radclive was an efficient hangman with a near-perfect record. He tried to improve his trade by introducing a method known as 'jerk'em up gallows'. Instead of dropping victims through the trap door as was customary, they would by pulled upward suddenly and left to hang. Radclive had to cease using this method after hanging Reginald Birchall. Birchall took 18 minutes to strangle to death.

In Quebec a condemned man fell dead in Radclive's arms prior to the hanging. The sheriff insisted that the man still be hung.

Radclive died in October, 1912 from health problems brought about by heavy drinking.

was a notorious individual who formed a club called the Black and Tans. This group of students roved the countryside on horseback and ravaged farms and villages for a thirty-mile radius.

By his third year of college he had spent his entire inheritance of 4,000 pounds. Reginald had lived like an English lord with several horses to his name and he drank and socialized to his heart's content. His debts in this university town to tailors, winesellers and other merchants were soon made known and his name was removed from the university rolls.

Birchall, enterprising and opportunistic, quickly landed a job stage-managing a road show. During this time he became familiar with revolvers. Actors demanding money could be put in their place with a gun. Needless to say the job did not last.

He tried the racetrack. This, too, failed. Birchall tried love next and eloped with a slender blond named Florence, the daughter of David Stevenson, a venerable and wealthy railway superintendent. Florence, of course, would be in line for a fortune. But Birchall couldn't wait; he wrote cheques on a non-existent bank account. Now he was in real trouble. A family council decided it was necessary to send the young Birchalls to Canada. Left to his own vices and devices, God only knew what Birchall would do. So the Birchalls emigrated under the auspices of an English firm, which had an agent, a retired farmer by the name of Macdonald, near Woodstock, Ontario, who received a commission by placing apprentices on farms in Oxford County.

Reginald and Florence spent their first night in Canada on a farm. The next morning he left that "human pigsty" as he called it, and gave up farming for life. The couple went to Woodstock as Lord and Lady Somerset, hoping to gain attention and social acclaim. They were a hit, especially among wealthy land owners who only dreamed of hobknobbing with the titled. The Birchalls resided in the area that autumn and throughout the winter. By early spring their debt load was high. As bill collectors advanced, the couple retreated to England.

There in England, Reginald Birchall dreamed up his next scheme. His own experience in Canada was inspiration for his next business venture. Birchall quickly placed his ad in numerous papers and waited for replies. Two men responded, Fred Benwell and Douglas Pelly.

Murray's case was developing nicely but he wasn't finished yet. He still needed a witness or two to place Birchall at or near the scene of the crime. Fate intervened, Douglas Pelly panicked and reported his suspicions to Thomas Young of the Ontario police. Young arrested the Birchalls on the strength of Pelly's statements. Detective Murray now had to work fast to build his case.

He needed to know if Birchall and Benwell had boarded a morning train bound for Windsor in February. His luck was with him. Conductor William H. Poole, of the Grand Trunk Railroad, recalled two passengers matching Murray's descriptions who left Niagara Falls on the morning train of February 17th. Poole told Murray they got off train at Eastwood, four miles from the Blenheim swamp, at 11:14 on the morning of the seventeenth.

Miss Lockhart, a passenger on that morning train, also confirmed that the two men had been seated a couple of rows behind her. She noticed them talking about the fields the train was passing through as they neared Eastwood. The older of the two, she said, wore a big astrakhan cap. She watched them disembark from the train and set out to the north. She said the man with the fur cap was in the lead.

Murray was fortunate to discover James Rapson who had been cutting timber with a crew of men less than a mile from Blenheim swamp that fateful date. He reported to Murray that he heard two pistol shots in rapid succession about one o'clock.

Approximately 2:30 p.m. that same day, one Charles Buck was returning home from Woodstock. At the crossroads leading to Eastwood, a stranger turned the corner from the Blenheim swamp road. He was wearing a fur cap. He asked for directions to Gobles Corners, stating he wished to go to Woodstock. Buck told the man he was within two miles of Eastwood and would get to Woodstock from there as quickly as from Gobles Corners. The man in the fur cap then set out for Eastwood at a quick pace.

Miss Alice Smith couldn't believe it when she ran into Lord Somerset at three o'clock that afternoon at the Eastwood Station. She had been well acquainted with his lordship during his last stay in the area. The two had a pleasant conversation, while Birchall purchased a train ticket. Miss Mary Swayzie, of Eastwood, had no idea who Birchall was but noted that his trousers were turned up and his shoes were muddy.

Two other witnesses spotted Lord Somerset boarding the train bound for Niagara Falls from Eastwood at 3:38, that afternoon.

Murray now was apprised of some essential circumstantial evidence. He wanted more proof. He wondered why Reginald Birchall and his wife returned to the district to identify Benwell. If he had not done so he would have never been a suspect; Douglas Pelly might have made it to the bottom of Niagara Falls and the Birchalls could have moved to another country, or continued to recruit and murder unsuspecting young Englishmen.

Reginald Birchall made yet another fatal mistake. On February 20th, three days after the death of Benwell, he wrote a letter to his father, Colonel Benwell, stating "I have been talking to your son today about arrangements, and he is so well satisfied with the prospects here that he is ready to go immediately into partnership." Birchall went on to ask for another 500 pounds. Although the letter wasn't dated, the envelope had been post-marked February 20. Upon hearing of his son's death Colonel Benwell sent the letter to the Canadian authorities. Murray was ready for trial.

Although it was conceivable that Mrs. Birchall was unaware of her husband's activities she was nonetheless acquitted as an accessary to the murder at the inquest. Perhaps she, too, had been hypnotized by his charm. Reginald was charged with the murder of Benwell.

In September of 1890, Reginald was brought to the Woodstock jail. Since the new courthouse was still under construction the trial took place in the town hall. To give the hall a courtroom appearance a carpeted dais was built just in front of the stage. The witness box was to the left and an area for the jury was to the right.

Mr. Justice MacMahon of Guelph presided over the trial. B.B. Osler, QC, was counsel for the crown and G.T. Blackstock, QC, was counsel for the defense. The criminal docket of the fall assizes that year was a busy one. There were two rape cases, a cattle poisoning and the murder trial, to name a few. The Birchall trial had what was described as a circus-like atmosphere. On the first day, Monday, September 22, 1890, 1,500 people crammed into the space in front of city hall, hoping to get in to see the trial or catch a glimpse of the prisoner. Woodstock itself only had a population of 9,400 residents at that time. Reginald Birchall was certainly the drawing card. He had such a way with people. He literally mesmerized everyone he met. He was a handsome chap

The real Reg Birchall (left) inspired copy-cats.

with a heavy black moustache and was always dressed to the nines. People were reluctant to believe him guilty. They simply wanted to forgive him. Women, it appeared, found him particularly beguiling.

Admittance to the court room was by ticket only and for the first time in Canadian court history the ladies turned out in full force to hear the proceedings. "In fact, the ladies are stepping beyond the bounds of good taste in their eagerness to attend trial sessions." according to *The Globe*.

The Globe also commented, "A notable feature of the trial is the great, and as some of the people seem to think, threatening increase of ladies. The reason for this is not quite clear. Probably it was

The courtroom before women were admitted. Birchall is in the dock, upper right.

deemed at first rather infra dig for ladies to attend the court unless they were of the fortunate few to be invited to seats upon the platform beside the bench, but if this is the case, either the ladies have discovered their mistake or else the curiosity of the sex has caused the point to be set aside by common consent. Yesterday some of the ladies discovered the gallery and took possession of it. Today these adventurous spirits were followed by so many others that the crowd overflowed to the floor, and during the exciting testimony of this afternoon the main body of the hall was occupied chiefly by ladies. There are those who fear that there will be no room for any men at the court room."

The trial was the coming of age for world communication in Canada. For the first time in Canadian newspaper history, direct telegraph lines were set up in a courtroom to send the story to papers across Canada, Great Britain, the United States, Germany, Italy and France.

London historian, Orlo Miller, wrote about the trial in his book entitled Twenty Mortal Murders, "John Wilson Murray had done his job well. The case he had prepared for the Crown was virtually air-tight. Nearly sixty witnesses were produced. The defense offered thirty-one witnesses and concentrated its attack on the credibility of some of the Crown's witnesses. The defense also endeavoured to prove that, in the vicinity of the Blenheim swamp, on the day of the crime, there were three transients who could have fired the fatal shots."

The defense also attempted to discredit the chronology of events, insisting that Birchall could not possibly have had enough time to travel from Niagara Falls to Eastwood, walk to the Blenheim Swamp, kill a man, return on foot to Eastwood and back to Niagara Falls by train the same day. However, Murray pointed out that according to the timetable Birchall had a total of four hours and twenty-four minutes to walk from the Eastwood station to the Blenheim swamp, to kill Benwell, and to return to Eastwood by three o'clock to catch the 3:38 train for Niagara Falls.

During the trial, Birchall, somewhat of an artist and ever the opportunist, made life-like sketches of those who testified against him. He hoped to sell the pen and ink drawings to newspapers or anyone of interest.

BIRCHALL'S OWN DRAWINGS

Birchall meditating

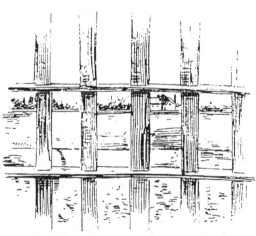

The west gaol yard viewed from Birchall's cell.

Mrs. Birchall and her sister Mrs. Wesley Jones (left).

Spectators held their gaze on Reginald Birchall, but also on two other figures, Mrs. Birchall and her sister, Mrs. Wesley Jones, both tall, slim women, elegantly dressed, their features concealed by heavy veils.

The trial lasted one week. Justice MacMahon delivered his charge to the jury, at eight o'clock on the evening of Monday, September 29, 1890. He finished his address shortly after ten o'clock. The jury returned to the hall about midnight with its verdict — guilty! All eyes were on Birchall, and in a solemn voice the judge commanded the prisoner to stand. Birchall did so promptly, his face drained of colour and he stood quite still. His eyes fixed steadily on the judge. His Lordship spoke low, but with a tremor in his voice as this was his first death sentence. "What have you to say, John Reginald Birchall, why the sentence of the court should not be pronounced on you for the felony of murder that you have committed?"

The prisoner looked more intently at the judge and said in a loud, clear voice, "Simply that I am not guilty of the crime, my lord."

The audience, too, was very still, very attentive.

His Lordship continued, "It is part of a solemn and painful duty to pass upon you the sentence of the court for the felony of which you have been convicted. I can only say I fully concur in the verdict which has been returned by the jury on the indictment against you.

You have been defended with great ability and there has been no point connected with the defense that has not been fully brought before the jury and pressed upon them with all the fervor and all the ability that human nature could command, and while I say that I may say also that the inevitable conclusion that has been reached in the minds not only of the jury but of almost every one who has listened to the trial was that you conceived and premeditated and carried out the murder of a young man who had been entrusted to you by an aged father. It was your duty and bounded duty to have looked after and protected him. Instead, you prepared to take his life and to reap the miserable reward that you thought was to be obtained by asking the price of the blood money which you would get by the draft that was to come from England. It is melancholy to think that after such a short period after you became a married man and became connected with an estimable and respectable family

Woodstock County gaol.

you should have brought this trouble and disgrace upon them. I can hold out to you no hope whatever of any commutation of the sentence I am about to pronounce. There is I may say to you, but a short time in which you can be permitted to live, and I earnestly implore you to take advantage of every hour that remains to make your peace by supplicating the Throne of Heavenly Grace for forgiveness of offenses committed by you in the flesh. The sentence of the court upon you, John Reginald Birchall, is that you be taken hence to the place whence you came, and that there within the walls of the prison between the hours of 8 o'clock in the morning and 6 in the afternoon on Friday, November 14 next, you be hanged by the neck until you are dead, and may the Lord have mercy on your soul."

Birchall sank back in his chair in the dock, while the spectators flocked around his box or passed over the top of the rail of the doomed man. He looked neither right nor left, but simply stared straight ahead. At 12:15 a.m. Birchall found himself back in his cell with a watch at the door. Mrs. Birchall had been sedated.

In his last days Birchall received flowers and telegrams from admirers. One *Globe* reporter wrote, "He has received a number of letters, telegrams and cablegrams. They are nearly all the ravings of persons who appeal to the officials to avert the execution in language that has at this late hour of their hero's life become hysterical and extravagantly threatening."

On November 12th, Birchall wrote an agreement made in duplicate between his jailer George Perry and Messrs. M.S. Robinson & Company of Toronto concerning his clothes and the right to exhibit his head, bust and figure after his death. According to one report Birchall had made arrangements to sell the clothes worn on the day of the murder of Benwell to the proprietors of "Wonderland."

The agreement read, "Whereas the said G.E. Perry is the duly authorized agent of J.R. Birchall, now confined in Woodstock Gaol, had the right to dispose of certain personal effects and rights belonging to the said Birchall. Said Perry for himself and said Birchall agree with said M.S. Robinson & Company in consideration of the sum of $150, to procure for and sell to said M.S. Robinson & Company the

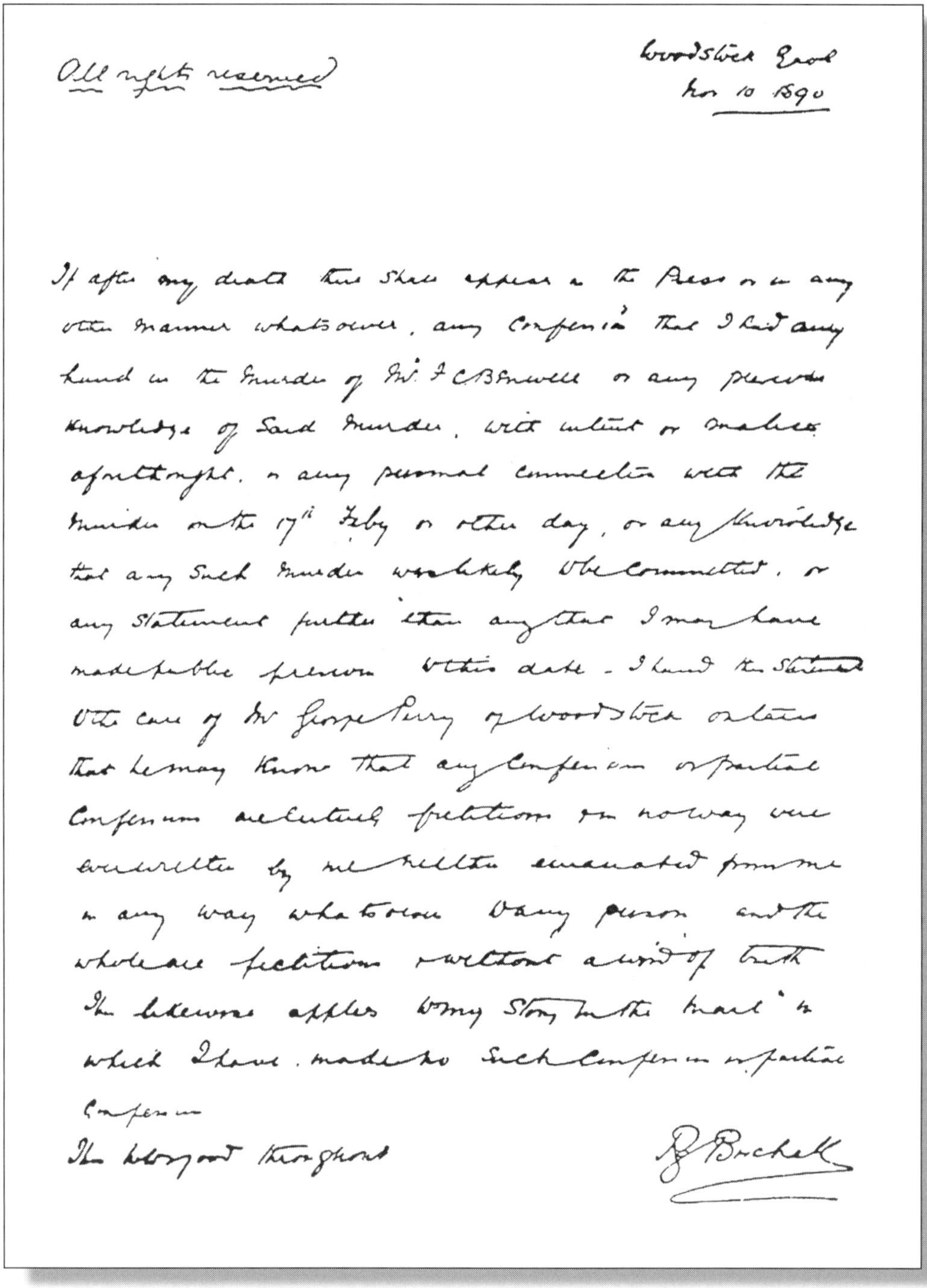

All rights reserved

Woodstock Gaol
Nov 10 1890

If after my death there shall appear in the Press or in any other manner whatsoever, any Confession that I had any hand in the Murder of Mr. F C Benwell or any previous knowledge of said Murder, with intent or malice afterthought, or any personal connection with the murder on the 17th Feby or other day, or any knowledge that any such murder was likely to be committed, or any Statement further than anything I may have made public previous to this date – I hand this Statement to the care of Mr George Perry of Woodstock on terms that he may know that any confession or partial confession are entirely fictitious or no way were ever written by me neither emanated from me in any way whatsoever to any person and the whole are fictitious or without a word of truth. The likewise applies to my Story in the trial in which I have made no such confession or partial confession.

The blotproof throughout

R Birchell

R. Birchall

HIS LAST WRITTEN STATEMENT

He Protests His Innocence of the Killing of Benwell.

BIRCHALL

clothing apparel and outfit, including all articles of dress worn by the said Birchall on the 17th February, 1890. Also a certain collection of sketches executed personally by said Birchall and the sole and exclusive right to exhibit a representation of the head, bust and figure in wax or other materials of the said Birchall in Toronto and elsewhere."

Detective Murray was still playing an active role in Birchall's life. On several occasions Murray visited Birchall in the Woodstock Gaol. Apparently Birchall held Murray in great esteem. During their last talk together Birchall addressed Murray, "I have found you, sir, always a gentleman. You did your duty. I have no hard feelings against you."

Murray knew from talking to Birchall that he had originally intended to throw his victim into Pine Pond, which was alleged to be bottomless, however the last time he and his wife had picnicked there and on the day of the murder, a fire and storm had ravaged the swamp, choking the way to the lake. The possibility of discovery of the body where Birchall had left it had been remote. The strange circumstance in connection with the discovery of the crime was that the swamp was navigable only from the day of the crime until all the evidence had been gathered.

Birchall's demeanor remained unchanged. "Birchall began to show an interest in the events of tomorrow (November 14) as though he were to have no personal concern in them. The scaffold was put up in the northeast corner of the west yard today. The spot almost directly under his cell window and while he could not see the operations he could hear the sound of the hammer. Unable to see the men at work, he grew curious and asked his day guard, George Perry, to draw him a design of the structure and explain its working. This Perry did and Birchall's simple remark was, 'My, but it is crude.'"

As the fatal hour approached Mrs Florence Birchall visited her husband for the last time. Her short stay was reported by the Toronto Mail newspaper, "She burst into a terrible fit of weeping and moaning aloud, and would insist upon returning and having a last look at her husband through the door. Birchall stood at the door, gazing long and lovingly down upon her, and as she turned back, waved his hand and said, 'Goodbye Flo. Don't take it too hard. God bless you'."

On the frosty morning of November 14, 1890, Reginald Birchall was led out into the jail yard in front of 50 reporters and medical men. A few metres from the scaffold two telegraph operators stood with instruments in their hands ready to wire to England the moment the drop fell. Some people reported that the hangman had not done his job properly and that Birchall, who should have died in seconds, actually strangled to death. His body was placed in a metal casket and buried in the northwest corner of the jail yard. For years rumors persisted that the burial was a fake. Where was Reginald Birchall really buried? In 1896, the corpse was exhumed and a reporter named Alf Rubbra from the *Woodstock Sentinel Review* claimed to be present and snipped a couple of wisps from Birchall's moustache as evidence. The body was again placed in its resting place.

Years later people in the district acknowledged the fact that they had useful articles made from the wood that had been taken from the spot where the murder was committed. Perhaps Joseph and George Eldridge hadn't forgotten their wood after all.

Just prior to his death Reginald Birchall left us with these words:

"The day of my execution
Was a pitiful sight to see.
Two of my chums from Montreal
Took their last farewell of me.
Now my song is nearly ended
I hope I've offended none.
And if I have, come tell me
Before I will be hung.
My wife she came to see me
The night before I died.
She threw her arms around me
And bitter she cried.
She said, My dearest husband
I fear that you shall die.
For the murder of Frederick Benwell
Upon the gallows high."

The Love-sick Doctor

*T*he stairs of the scaffold creaked beneath the feet of the murderer. Each step drew the crowd of 10,000 closer to their belief in justice and the day of reckoning. Onlookers were mesmerized by the hangman's noose swinging gently in the warm spring breeze. Many people had travelled many days and many miles to capture this moment in their memory. They wanted to experience the sight of death. As the noose was slipped around the neck of the convict a young woman fainted in her brothers arm's, others audibly sighed, a sea of heads swayed back and forth when the body began to swing in the air. For half an hour they stood there as the shadow of death claimed its due. With bizarre satisfaction, spectators including relatives of the deceased, cut the hangman's rope into souvenirs the moment the corpse was cut down.

This story begins in 1833, on a farm just outside Brighton, Ontario, where a baby boy was born, a boy named William Henry King. William was a keen learner and at age 5 was sent to school. By age 18, he was in Toronto attending teacher-training college. During the summers he would return home to work on the family farm.

William was a handsome man, five feet eleven inches tall, with a full head of hair and sandy whiskers. His stature commanded the attention of young ladies. One summer in Brighton he started to date a young woman by the name of Sarah Ann Lawson. The ladies of Brighton were disappointed. Sarah Ann was not a particularly pretty woman. She had a stern countenance and a reputation for frowning with her eyebrows raised. Some folks wondered if William King was after the Lawson fortune. It was a fact that Mr. John M. Lawson was a prosperous farmer and a well-respected man in the community. No one in the Lawson family showed concern for this idle gossip. On January 31, 1855, Sarah and William married.

William continued his studies and earned a first-class teacher's certificate in Toronto. Sarah supported her husband faithfully and even took in boarders to help defray his educational costs.

When William started his first teaching job they seemed destined to live the good life, but one never knows what life has in store. Sarah was in the family way — a cause for celebration. Unfortunately the tiny infant was destined to live a short life and the Kings buried their first child only one month later.

Soon rumours of physical abuse in the King household began to surface. The only evidence of their unhappiness was that Sarah left William and returned home to live with her parents. Although there was gossip about this abuse there could have been many reasons for Sarah's return to her parents. What is known as fact is that William returned to his studies and Sarah's father paid the tab with a loan.

William enrolled in Philadelphia's Homeopathy Medical College. There he attended school for three years, only returning home during the summer months until he graduated as a doctor.

One semester William wrote several letters to his wife in which he accused her of infidelity. What was that all about? Sarah immediately showed the letters to her father who in turn submitted them to his lawyer. When William heard all of this, he apologized and his father-in-law returned the letters to him, but not before he made copies of them.

Now William needed to tread more softly. If he was no longer happy with his marriage very few people really knew about it. Shortly after he graduated from medical school in 1858, he returned to Brighton where they set up house and a medical practice. Each night he returned home to his beloved wife. All seemed in order.

King professed to love his wife but said he wanted her to elevate herself to a level befitting a doctor's wife. She came from a wealthy family, yet Sarah was a country girl at heart. She had no interest in possessing the virtues associated with a sophisticated society and she could not change her personality. This disappointed King. He once remarked to a friend, "Though she is a good wife to get money, I would like to see her improved in many respects."

The *Cobourg Sentinel* reported that although prosperous in business, he was a failure at home. His pent-up frustration sought some form of release and he turned his attention to other women. He attempted an affair with one Miss Garrett who would have nothing to do with him. Her rejection added to his depression.

In the late summer of 1858, Sarah took a fall while dismounting a carriage. As a result she was confined to bed. Despite William's ministerings, Sarah's condition deteriorated. Occasionally she would rally and then slip back into a state of helplessness.

That same year, William met and fell in love with Miss Melinda Vandervoort of the nearby township of Sidney, in Hastings County. She was an acquaintance of Sarah's and one day came to visit. William himself described the moment, "I happened to be home, and after having received an introduction to her, I soon engaged in conversation, and finding her to be a very intelligent young lady, (twenty-years-old) we became quite intimate. She remained about 4 hours until near evening. I got my horse up and drove her and my wife down to my father-in-law's, where we stayed for about an hour. When we left my wife said to me, 'Miss. Vandervoort says she has fallen in love with you. She loved you before she ever saw you'."

William couldn't help himself, he had to write Miss Vandervort a letter expressing how he felt. She replied by sending him a photograph of herself and a letter stating, "You have unlinked the tender cord of affection until you have an alarming influence over my girlish nature. One smile from your countenance can inspire a depth of veneration in my bosom never felt by me for any individual."

They continued their secretive romance. William was spellbound. He later stated, "Oh! How I wish she had not fired the fatal dart in my heart. Oh! That fatal moment when our hearts met. She is the most precious of Earth's pearls, the star of my existence."

William followed his own convictions, "My doctrine of the philosophy of human nature has always been this; that every heart has the object of its affections somewhere in the opposite sex, and then whenever two people meet, that object will be made known to them by intuition."

But what about Sarah?

The tombstone marks the grave site of Sarah Ann King and her first child.

William continued to write Melinda and to express his thoughts about his ailing wife. He asked her to be patient and wait, for Sarah could die at any moment. In no time at all she could be the next Mrs. King!

Meanwhile, Sarah's condition was rapidly deteriorating. Melinda, when she wasn't riding around with Dr. King, would come to the house and attend to her. Although people gossiped about Dr. King and Melinda, no one was suspicious of the ultimate consequences of that liaison. Sarah was vomiting continuously, and suffering from excruciating pains in her stomach. She often complained of a burning sensation in her throat and she was, once again, two months pregnant!

On the days when Sarah was feeling better she begged her husband to stop giving her that white powder five times a day. She complained that it "burned like fire" in her mouth.

Dr. King admitted publicly that his wife's present condition was in no way related to the fall from the carriage. In fact, he diagnosed her, with ulcerations of the stomach and intestinal irregularities, as having Cholera morbus. An acute, infectious, epidemic disease, Cholera morbus is characterized by serious intestinal disorders caused by bacterium. It was fatal.

Sarah's father John Lawson insisted William seek out a second medical opinion. William abliged by calling in Dr. A.E. Fife. Dr. Fife was informed by William that the patient was pregnant and suffered from ulcerations of the womb. For whatever reason (perhaps the infectious nature of the disease?) Dr. Fife did not examine Sarah, instead he prescribed ipecacuanha and camphor to alleviate the vomiting.

The medicine didn't help and Sarah's condition continued to deteriorate. Her father was beside himself. He begged William to ask for additional medical assistance. Dr. P. Gross was then contacted. He received the same information from William that Dr. Fife had been given. Once again Mrs. King was not examined by the doctor. He too, prescribed some medicine to help stem the persistent vomiting.

At one point Sarah's mother showed William some black spots from a discharge on Sarah's night gown. He ordered her to burn the garment, warning her that she might become infected if she had a scratch on her hand. She refused and William proceeded to cut out the spots with scissors and to dispose of the cloth.

According to William, Sarah knew the score, she was pain-wracked, she knew that she and the child inside her were doomed. She used the last bit of her failing strength to confront him. "You're engaged to her. You're to be married to that girl.

"Oh! Lord, take me out of this world that I don't want to live in."

On November 7, Sarah Ann Lawson King and her unborn child were buried in the Brighton cemetery. William publicly grieved to such an extent some people believed he might take his own life. The Lawson family mourned for the loss of a loved one.

Mrs. Lawson was not convinced that her daughter died of natural causes. The following day she waited for William to leave the house and then she went in to search for some incriminating evidence. She was not sure what she might find but her intuitive nature told her that William had murdered her daughter. She readily discovered letters from Miss Melinda Vandervoort to William in his coat pockets. Murder seemed the obvious conclusion.

The Lawsons took these letters and copies of the ones written to Sarah by William when he was in medical school to the officials. An inquest was held to determine the cause of death. On November 8,

Sarah's body was exhumed, a coroner's jury empanelled and the inquest held in the nearby county schoolhouse. The body was placed on a door for the post mortem examination conducted by Drs. P.R. Proctor and P. Gross, of Brighton, and Dr. James Gilchrist, of Cobourg. Dr. Proctor observed, "The body presented a rather healthy appearance for one deceased. Body and organs were all in a healthy condition except lungs which presented a congested appearance but not sufficient to cause death. Womb contained a healthy foetus. Bowels and rectum colored as if inflamed from something which had passed through them. Surface of stomach congested - condition scarcely amounted to inflammation, it was a state of engorgement. A dark fluid was found inside the stomach."

Dr. Gross added, "I did not discover any signs of ulceration in the neck of the womb."

The Daily Globe of Toronto reported the autopsy of Mrs. King. "At the inquest, November 8th, the stomach and contents were removed in the presence of the jury and placed in a clean earthen dish. No one besides the doctors touched it (stomach). From this they were transferred to a pickle bottle. The mouth of the bottle was covered with paper which was tied down with string. It was then taken to Brighton where it was locked in a bureau.

"Next day, the jury having adjourned over by their consent, the stomach was returned to the schoolhouse where the inquest was held and was placed in a clean dish in the presence of the jury, as Drs. Gross and Proctor wished to see it again, the post mortem having been performed by candlelight.

"The stomach remained in the dish about 15-20 minutes. It was then returned to the bottle and corked, sealed in the presence of the jury, stamped with a penny piece, wrapped, sealed again, placed in a carpet bag and given to a member of the group to take to Queen's College, Kingston, for analysis."

For some unknown reason Queen's College refused to conduct the analysis and the carpet bag with Sarah's remains was returned to Brighton. From there it was shipped to The University of Toronto for examination by the chemistry department.

The results took a few days, but the verdict was simple: arsenic in the stomach and liver. Professor Henry Croft of the University stated, "Arsenic cannot be put into the liver after death. It must have been taken during life."

A summons was issued for William's arrest, but he was gone!

Mr. Lawson had unwittingly prepared William when he said the law would soon be on his trail. William fled to Melinda's home where he asked permission to speak with her privately. He explained that his wife was dead and that a picture of Melinda's likeness in his pocket would be cause enough for their arrest. Melinda's father agreed that the best course of action would be a trip to the states to visit Melinda's aunt. By the time the Sherriff arrived, they were long-gone.

The next events were told in court by Sarah's brother Clinton, "The coroner gave me a warrant to arrest Dr. King. I went to Kingston and from thence to Cape Vincent, across the river in New York State. I went six or eight miles up the country to a house kept by a man named Bate.

"Gordon, the United States marshal went into the house. I stopped before I got there, so that I might not be seen. He had been there three minutes when Dr. King jumped out of the window. I ran after him. He ran towards the woods, but as I was after him quick, he turned into a barn. We went in and found him under the straw in a hog's nest. I had a revolver; I said he must be shot if he ran. A lawyer told me I had no right to take him, and told King so, too."

Illegal or otherwise, King did not argue about the absence of extradition laws in the face of a pistol. He had two choices - death or a fair trial. He returned to Brighton and then to Cobourg where he was placed in the county jail. Melinda Vandervoort returned to Brighton three weeks later.

On April 4, 1859, the King trial began. *The Cobourg Star* described the event, "The Courthouse building was kept closed during the day, and persons were admitted only through a private door, yet in a short time, the room which will accommodate about four hundred people, was filled to excess, and a much larger crowd went away without getting in at all.

"The excitement throughout the country as well as the town

was intense. Several ladies from the town came up in the morning, but when they saw the crowd at the courthouse, returned again, judging very wisely that this was not the place to wear hoops. It was estimated that there were not less than fifteen hundred persons who came to hear the trial, and among them was a large number of medical men, and all the students from Victoria College."

At half past nine William King was brought into the court. He walked with a firm stride and an air of confidence. He declared himself not guilty of murder.

The crown prosecutor opened the trial. The jury was reminded that this case was extremely serious in nature. A Mr. Galt Q.C. for the crown began his address. He declared that King was the sole murderer of his wife. The motive for the murder was the love affair between King and Miss Vandervoort. His presentation was eloquent. "If the prisoner be found guilty, another instance will be added to those already on record wherein a knowledge of medicine has been put to the worst possible purpose - wherein the physician has cruelly, persistently and remorselessly used his skill for the destruction of life under the pretense of saving - wherein the husband has stood by the bedside of his dying wife and while speaking words of comfort to her, has betrayed her to a gradual and painful death..."

The defense counsel attempted to prove that the stomach was not handled in an appropriate manner and that poison could have been introduced after death. The question arose to whether arsenic had a cumulative effect and if so, was such an effect consistent with the innocence of the prisoner, the small amount of inflammation apparent in the stomach, and the absence of purging in the case, from beginning to end of the illness.

Coroner Davidson did admit that the bottle containing the stomach had not been sealed, or even corked, until the second day after its removal.

Professor Henry Croft of Toronto's University College testified that Sarah's stomach contained 11 grains of arsenic. Her liver showed moderate quantities of the substance. Croft pointed out that arsenic could not be placed into the liver after death.

Concerning the usage of arsenic as a remedial medicine, Professor Charles Hempel, M.D., of the Homoeopathic College of Pennsylvania, stated, "The gist of homoeopathic practice is this - for the cure of disease we administer medicines which, if taken by a healthy person, would produce a like disease. Arsenic is frequently used in homoeopathic practice. I believe arsenic to be a cumulative poison. I believe Mrs. King died from cumulative doses of arsenic."

Dr. Hempel also testified that he was dissatisfied with the medical testimony, and that the doctors who examined Mrs. King's body displayed considerable ignorance.

A Dr. Hodder's testimony was quite controversial. "I consider arsenic a very safe medicine. I have continued it in doses for two months, with occasional intermissions. It is not therefore a cumulative poison."

It was William King's defense and claim as a doctor that the use of arsenic was a professional decision, and not a criminal act. By choosing that line of defense he could potentially enjoy a new woman, a new life and freedom.

The jury had much to consider about arsenic and intent. Had he not caught her when she fell from the carriage, been present at her bedside every night caring for her, grieved her mortally after her death?

The crown was relentless. They put Sarah's mother on the stand. She tearfully testified that she watched William mix a white powder with water and administer it to her daughter. She watched her daughter vomit and retch after each dose. She also stated that Sarah's condition seemed to improve slightly at times.

Melinda Vandervoort also testified at the trial. "I never had any improper intercourse with Dr. King."

When asked to explain the photograph of herself she denied any relationship with William. "Mrs. King asked me to send the likeness to her. I directed the likeness to Dr. King. I thought that when I got the letter from him, it was written for amusement. I sent him this letter in answer for amusement."

Their correspondence was laid bare. William: "Sweet little lump of good nature. Could I indulge in the hope that those winning and genial smiles would ever be found in my possession, all troubles would then cease. It is a perfect infatuation to me. Can you keep from sacrificing yourself upon the hymeneal altar for the next year? I wish so."

Melinda, in response: "Since I first had the pleasure of an introduction, my heart is constantly with you, and I'm not contented a moment. O could I forever be with you; I think I should be happy,

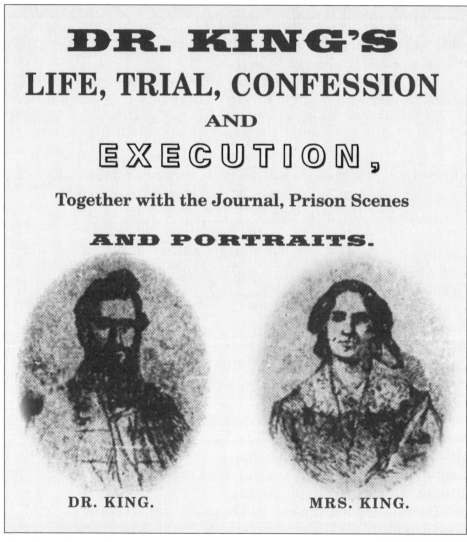

Dr. King's Pamphlet

for indeed I enjoyed myself to excess during my stay in your presence though suppose now I must eradicate such thoughts from my mind; for you are married, and my destiny must be to love and not share your interesting society."

Some jury members actually found the letters to be amusing under the circumstances. Others obviously thought they were enough to convict him of murder.

The jury retired at 3 p.m. to discuss the fate of William King. By the end of the day they still had not come to consensus. They were locked up for the night. The following morning at 10 a.m. they returned to court with a verdict. When the clerk of the court asked, "How say you, gentlemen, is the prisoner guilty or not guilty?" The foreman replied, "Guilty, with a strong recommendation to mercy."

On Saturday, April 9, William King was led back into the Cobourg courtroom. Chief Justice Burns asked William if he had anything to say before being sentenced. He replied, "I have this much to say, that upon my solemn oath I am not guilty of the charge laid against me. I have no doubt of this; my conscience is perfectly clear upon this point." The judge, however, refused to comply with the jury's recommendation for mercy. William King was to be hanged on Thursday, June 9. With all of that William's countenance fell and he wept.

For two months King remained silent, but ultimately he confessed. No one knows for sure whether it was friends or family who pressured him into admitting his guilt. Was it conscience, fear of hell or the desire for notoriety that led him to make a confession and to subsequently have it published in *The Globe*?

"It has been suggested that I gave her poisonous doses of arsenic to cause her sickness. Now I must solemnly declare and will do so the moment before I expect to meet my God that I never gave her one particle of arsenic until after her Cholera morbus was fully developed.

"Here I may observe that the whole scientific world are deceived in reference to the cause of death. She died from anaesthetic effects of chloroform, and not from anything else as many have supposed.

"Now there was a temptation I could not resist. No one else was around. She was already ill and would not survive anyway."

William asked Sarah if she would take anything herself to end her life and she was happy to do so.

The temptation overcame him as he heard a voice inside that assured him he would not be guilty and even suggested 'chloroform.'

Unable to sleep that night William paced back and forth. He thought he was going mad. By the morning of November 4, 1858, he had made a decision. He entered Sarah's room and applied the chloroform. It had the desired effect. "But O! What an awful feeling I had then. How I repented, but alas, it was too late. I just began to realize what had been done. Oh! The bitter pangs that I experienced cannot be imagined. The devil had me headlong into difficulty, but now came the remorse of conscience. Oh! How sharp, how pun-

Old Cobourg Courthouse where the hanging took place.

gent! I felt like death, and thought I would die."

A pamphlet entitled *"Dr. King's Life, Trial, Confession and Execution"* was published and sold a month later.

The Port Hope Weekly newspaper published a response to King's confession the next day. "We are tired of these penitential exhibitions. There is not a criminal about to suffer death, but is heralded as converted; so that it becomes almost a certain mode of securing salvation at the eleventh hour, to poison a wife, to cut the throat of a neighbor, or blow out somebody's brains. There is something repugnant in these conversions on compulsion, as if the hangman's rope were a more effective agency to reclaim the incorrigible, than the precepts of Christianity from the most eloquent preacher."

At 4 a.m. on the morning of June 9, 1859, William King rose from bed and ate a hearty breakfast. Afterwards he sat in prayer with the Reverend Vanderburg of Codrington. A few close friends were then allowed to visit King for the last time. By eight-thirty, almost ten thousand people, including women and children, had gathered around the gallows to watch the hanging of William King. Some wished to distance themselves from the event and so chose to picnic a short way from the scene. Many spectators had spent two days walking from Brighton to Cobourg to witness the hanging. Others read the advertisement of the event in papers throughout North America and had arrived by train.

At approximately 8:45 a.m. William King was led out of the jail by Sheriff Fortune and then ascended the steps leading to the scaffold platform. King faced the crowd and began an address in a clear voice. "My fellow Christians: I stand before you to-day in the most awful position in which a human being can be placed, convicted of the most dreadful of all crimes and sentenced by the laws of my country to pay the penalty of my guilt by sacrificing my own life.

"It is hard to be deprived of life in comparative youth: but I do not find fault with the most righteous dispensations of an all-wise providence." Several groans were heard from the crowd. One man yelled, "Get on with it." Another spectator called out, "What about your wife?" No one seemed interested in hearing King justify his evil deed. They wanted to see him hanging from a rope.

When King finished, the hangman, whose face was covered with a mask, approached him, fastened his hands behind his back, ordered him to kneel on the "drop" and tied his feet together. A white cap was then drawn over his face. As the ministers recited the prayer, the sheriff signaled the hangman. He withdrew the bolt holding the trap door and King quickly dropped a distance of six feet before the rope stopped his fall and broke his neck.

Some women fainted, others stared. The body was left hanging from the scaffold for more than half an hour.

Eventually William King was cut down and his parents placed his body in a casket and took it away. In those days a hanged man could not be buried in consecrated ground. His body was transported to the family farm in Codrington and buried at the edge of the

Dr. King is buried in this grove of trees.

property. A marker was placed at the site. Some time later a relative removed the headstone to prevent tourists from visiting the grave.

The life of Melinda Vandervoort tells the tale of love gone wrong. She left, shortly after the trial, for New York with yet another lover and shortly thereafter with another to Montreal. When none of these worked out she returned, broken-hearted, to Brighton. Few people associated with her there and she turned to alcohol. Nothing seemed to ease her troubled and guilty mind and by the 1890's she passed away in an asylum for the insane in Toronto.

This is what William concluded about his marriage and his lover: "The law may compel man and wife to live together, but I defy it to compel them to love each other. Oh! how lamentable beyond description that so much misery and unhappiness should arise from unhappy marriages–Oh! woman! Oh! wine! Oh money! Three roots to evil in the world. All useful when properly used, but dangerous when abused.

"To every man who contemplates marriage at some future time, I would say take a glance over the last five years of my life and see where my misfortunes began–in marriage.

"Had I never seen her (Miss Vandervoort), I should not be where I am. She has cost me my life, which is all any man could pay for a woman. Oh! what a precious jewel. What a dear creature!"

The King homestead still stands in Codrington. Somewhere in a clump of lilacs on that property lies the remains of William King.

The Great Parry Sound Train Robbery

*I*t was a warm, still and misty night on Saturday August 18, 1928 when the southbound no. 4 locomotive pulled several coaches and a mail car along the C.P.R. steel tracks from Sudbury, Ontario. No one at the time would have guessed that this particular train would soon be involved in fatal gunplay.

A Parry Sound train just like this was held up in 1928.

A beam of moonlight silently penetrated the low-hanging clouds to reveal three ghostly figures advancing towards the tracks. A distant whistle sounded as the train neared Romford Station. With linesmen's belts secured at their waists and steel climbing spurs strapped to their boots, the men waited for the approaching iron beast. As the train passed around a curve they grasped the side of a swaying coach and, cat-like, scrambled to the roof and made for the mail car. As the train passed the junction they pulled large black stockings over their heads. At the crucial moment the robbers swung down from the roof through the open mail-car door. Loaded revolvers were pointed at the three startled clerks who guarded the mail, and as was later testified, one hooded gunman barked out the orders, "If you guys don't want to get hurt, just keep quiet and stand in the corner over there. That's right. Now turn around, face the wall and stay that way, see? One wrong move and the three of you'll get it!"

Another man quickly tore open registered letters, pocketed the money and took one mail bag.

As the train drew slowly into Parry Sound, the robbers knew that time was short to make their escape. They jumped and disappeared into the nighttime shadows.

Shortly after 3 a.m. Mrs. Robert Laird of Gibson Street, near to the Parry Sound Train station, was awakened by the noise of a vehicle in their driveway. Mrs. Laird was horrified to see her visiting brother-in-law's Studebaker coupe head out of town. Her husband, Haughton, and his brother, Walter, set out in hot pursuit along with their boarder, Harold J. Rolland, in his car.

Although the thieves were nearly fifteen minutes ahead of them, they managed to follow the tire tracks which were clearly visible on the moistened gravel roads of Parry Sound and onto the old Northern Colonization Road (now known as Highway 124) about ten miles outside of Parry Sound. Could they catch them?

Meanwhile, a young girl named Blanche Grant was dreaming of stars bursting and of diamonds cracking when she awoke to realize that someone was throwing pebbles at her window. Blanche recorded her early memories of that morning in a story entitled 'The Great Parry Sound Train Robbery Caper', "We lived in the C.P.R.

Nobel station (just north of Parry Sound) where my father was the agent. I was only eleven at the time. I woke Father. I said, 'There is a trainman at my window. He said the No. 4 has been robbed. 'Dad was out of bed in a hurry and stormed to my room. He called out, 'Who robbed what?'

"The trainman yelled up, 'Mornin', Sedge. Someone's just robbed the No. 4.'

"'D'you know it's three in the morning?' bellowed my father.

"'They still robbed the train. I saw a masked bandit with a bag climbing down the mailcar.'

"My father ran out, started his car, jumped from it, rushed back into the house, grabbed his shotgun from the cabinet, and raced over to get A.P. Cummings who lived in the house behind us. My father and A.P. drove away, their guns sticking out from the turned-down windows of Dad's car. They said they would cut the robbers off at the pass, a spot where the Nobel Road intersects with Hwy. 124, because, in their opinion, the robbers would try to escape towards North Bay.

"I said to my sister, 'This is exciting. It's just like a wild west story. Dad and A.P. will get more men, form a posse and then they will hunt down the bandits and when they get them… They'll hang them from the nearest tree.'"

No one knew the number of occupants in the stolen car. Were they car thieves or were they actually the train robbers? If so, the Laird boys had no idea who they were really following, nor what lay ahead.

In those days Highway 124 was a narrow winding road, not too unlike today, and quite hazardous for a speedy drive at night. Evidently the stolen coupe missed the bend and slid into a ditch near a bridge a short distance from the village of Waubamik. One of the car thieves set out for help to a nearby farmhouse owned by the Jackson family.

Shortly before 4 a.m. 62-year-old Thomas Jackson was awakened by a knock at the front door. Thomas rose from bed and went to see who it could be. Upon opening the door he was greeted by a stranger.

"I've come from the United States and not knowing the highway I went off the road just down the way. Could you help me?" asked the man.

Thomas was a likeable and well respected farmer. His pioneering nature always guided him to help anyone in need.

He told the man to wait while he woke up his younger son, Claude, to help harness the horses.

At the scene of the accident father and son saw an unoccupied car with Ohio license plates crashed lamely in a hollow. They hooked up a chain to pull the car out. The first attempt failed. Then the stranger jumped into the car, started the motor and turned on the headlights. Just as Thomas was about to lead the horses again, his attention was drawn to a vehicle approaching from the west. It was the Laird brothers and Harold Rolland.

When the approaching men spotted the stolen car they decided to plan a strategy before approaching the vehicle.

After all, car thieves could be armed. So they breezed by and pulled over a few hundred yards past the ditched car.

Rolland was the first to ask the question, "What will we use for weapons?"

Walter glanced around the car and spotted the tool box. Haughton opened the lid and grabbed a wrench.

"This will do," he said.

Walter took a piece of iron and Rolland grabbed an extension for

THOMAS JACKSON

the jack. Now the trio were ready to apprehend the bandit or bandits. They walked back down the road under the cover of darkness.

As they neared the stranded coupe they caught sight of Claude Jackson standing by the horses. Walter informed Claude that the car was stolen, while Haughton eyed a stranger who was sitting behind the wheel. Thomas Jackson was standing near the rear of the car. Overcoming his fear, Haughton walked up to the side of the car, hopped onto the running board and leaned in the window.

"Having trouble? Need any help?" Haughton inquired.

A curt "no" was the response.

Desperate Struggle Outside the Jackson Farm

BANDIT CAPTURED BY BRAVE YOUTHS

"I accuse you of stealing this car. You're under arrest," shouted Haughton.

Turning to Walter, Haughton yelled, "Put the gun on him."

Walter quickly jumped onto the running board and drew the wrench out of his pocket.

"Don't shoot," cried the stranger.

"Raise your hands and get out of the car," shouted Haughton.

Slowly sliding across the leather seat to the far side of the car the stranger climbed out. Before anyone could turn their heads he dashed behind the car. He crouched down, pulled a .45-calibre pistol from his pocket, took aim and pulled the trigger. Four sharp cracks rang out in rapid succession.

The first or perhaps the second bullet struck Haughton. Another slug found its mark in Walter's chest. It was total chaos. Suddenly more shots were heard from the forest. It was an ambush. One bullet struck the sharp edge of the steel frame of the Studebaker's rear window and ricochetted.

Walter could feel the adrenalin rushing through his veins. His fear had turned to a wild rage. Despite his wound he lunged at the gunman. The force of his body knocked the culprit down. Another shot rang out, but the bullet hit the mud.

Haughton rushed to Walter's aid and struck the gunmen a sharp blow to the head with his wrench. He sat on the unconscious man until some rope could be found.

It was Haughton who saw Thomas Jackson staggering up the laneway with his hands over his face and he called out, "What's wrong with Jackson?"

Rolland and Walter rushed to his aid.

Thomas was in trouble. A wound to his neck looked serious and he was gasping for air.

The Colt automatic pistol used during the deed.

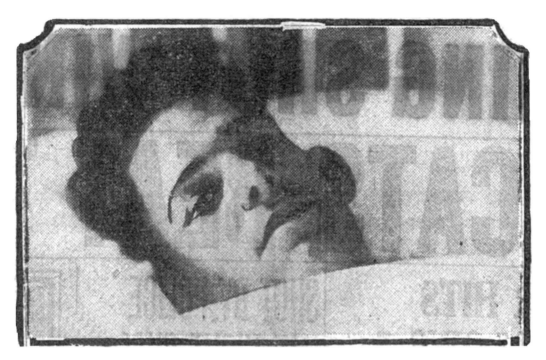

Walter Laird in hospital bed.

The boys led him up to the farm.

A few minutes later Haughton and Claude entered the farmhouse with the prisoner, now bound. Claude rushed to his father's side. Haughton handed the gun over to Walter. The captured man's pockets revealed a handkerchief with four clips of bullets, all of them .45 calibre and matching the Colt automatic pistol.

Constable R.G. Beatty of Parry Sound arrived on the scene and began to investigate the full details of what had just happened. Beatty went over to the couch to question Thomas Jackson but one look told him he was too late. Thomas was dead. John Burowski, the car thief, possible murderer and train robber was transported to the Parry Sound District Jail under the watchful eye of jailer Thomas Keating. There he awaited a court hearing.

By the early morning hours of August 18th, 1928, the townspeople awoke to discover a flood of Toronto reporters. Scores of journalists from The Daily Star, *The Daily Mail and Empire, The*

Evening Telegram and a host of other publications jammed the roadways. According to Adrian Eric Hayes, in his newspaper article of August 25, 1989, entitled, "Murder Filled Town With National Reporters", "Reporters came for the details of a story that included all of the elements necessary to tantalize readers, including a villain, an armed robber, gun-play, local heroes, a car chase, and the inevitable murder."

The Toronto Star reported, "Dawn broke to-day over a scene of brutal violence and tragedy but the first warm rays of the rising sun found more than two score of men afield, combing the surrounding dense bush with rifles in hand and revolvers at hip for an unknown.

Inspector John Miller (left) examines the windshield where the bullet supposedly ricocheted and struck Thomas Jackson.

Since the first alarm no time has been lost in the endeavor to run down the second culprit involved in the mail robbery's grim aftermath. Federal, Provincial and local police, guards from the Burwash Reformatory and enraged citizens from the surrounding countryside, all armed, have been out in the bush."

Blanche Grant awaited her father's return. To her it seemed as long as a schoolyear. When he did return he was discouraged that he had seen no robbers and was involved in no western-style heroics. Miss

Armed posse members take time out from the search for bandits to pose for a photograph in front of the Parry Sound C.P.R. station.

Grant writes, "I was disappointed too. Before noon a big man hunt was on and I saw gas-powered jiggers driving up and down the track. Guns owned by determined men stuck out from these little railcars that were so noisy that I said to myself, 'If I were a robber I'd have plenty of time to hole up or climb a tree or hide in a fallen log before the jiggers would come into sight.'"

The search was on for the other train robbers. Before the day ended 25 provincial officers under the direction of Inspector John Miller of Toronto, eight specially sworn citizens and several police officers from both railroads and the Salvation Army were searching the bush. Motor cars bearing officers travelled over the highways of the district. An area of nearly 125 miles was under constant supervision. Every train that passed through the district was searched.

The Toronto Star reported, "A man with a hacking cough, about five feet ten inches, wearing a short mustache, is about all of the clues to the fugitive. His alleged partner in crime (Burowski) refuses to divulge any further particulars which might lead to his identification." How many robbers were there?

Superintendent of railway mail services, A.M. Gibson, stated: "Our mail clerks were held up with their backs to the wall of the car while the bandits looted the mails. The distance between the point where the robbers entered the car and where they made their exit was about 30 miles."

Sightings poured in. One report said a man answering the description had been spotted boarding a freight train at Bayswater. Some people thought he left the train in the vicinity of Key Junction, Mowat or Pickeral. Searching the train proved unproductive.

By now nine vagrants had been picked up for questioning and were lodged in the Parry Sound jail by provincial police officers. Several more tramps living by the tracks outside Parry Sound were eventually charged with vagrancy or trespassing and were jailed. The total hit 40 before the hunt was over. Twenty-two jail cells accommodated the would-be culprits.

Police officials frantically felt the need to find someone. Was it media or public pressure? One quiet man by the name of Shorty who lived in Noble might have thought so. He was questioned by Inspector Mitchell and two constables. Shorty refused to reveal his true name and, as a result, they charged him with vagrancy, cuffed him and transported him to jail.

Shorty had lived in the area for several years. The newspapers quickly reported that no one knew how he earned his living, since they had not seen him go to work in some years. He was also Polish, the same nationality as Burowski! The police believed that somebody with a strong knowledge of the district was in league with the mail robbers. They believed Shorty might be the man.

The Evening Telegram reported, "While Shorty may not have been one of the gang who carried out the robbery, he may have supplied them with information leading up to it. It is also believed he may have been the man directing it."

It was reported that footprints had been discovered near the stolen car leading into the bush. However, further investigation was unsuccessful. The robbers continued to evade the authorities.

According to journalist Adrian Eric Hayes Hayes in his article entitled, 'After the killing near Waubamik...', "The strongest clue to the identity and whereabouts of the train robbers was reported to police officials Monday morning by a 17 year-old, Edward Welsh. The Welsh family resided three miles from Parry Sound on the opposite side of the town from where the Jackson house is located. Edward recalled, 'Around eight o'clock on Saturday morning two men came up to our house. Dad is a constable and he was away at the time.

'When they got outside the gate they dropped a canvas bag that looked similiar to the bags they use on mail cars. They left it there, came in and asked for something to eat. We were afraid that they would hold us up, so mother gave them something.

'They said they had slept in the bush all night. They were wet from rain and looked tired out and as if they had had a rough trip. It took them only a few minutes to gobble their food and then they disappeared down the road in a decided hurry in the direction of the heavier bush.

'All the time the men were talking to us one of them kept pulling his sweater down as if to hide something in his pocket. I thought then that he might have had a gun.'"

On the same day the *Toronto Star* stated, "The belief is spreading about the district that the hunted men are no longer in the bush but have escaped and are already across the border. Police admit this is possible."

The next day *The Star* addressed Jackson's death, "Today a little frame farmhouse was enveloped in sorrow and a black drape upon the closed door was evidence of the grim reaper's visit. Inside lay the body of the farmer who paid with his life for unwittingly trying to assist the escape of the two men who a couple of hours earlier robbed the mail car of the Vancouver-Toronto C.P.R. express while the train was en route between Sudbury and Toronto."

That afternoon the three mail clerks, Macdonald, Clarke and Doyle entered the bleak walls of the county jail in hopes of identifying the mail-car bandits. The clerks pinpointed Burowski as a suspect.

On Monday morning, August 20, 1928 in the absence of Magistrate J.D. Broughton, Justices of Peace C.C. Johnson, Mayor of Parry Sound and Frank Cook, ex. mayor, occupied the bench when

The accused John Burowski prior to facing the jury.

John Burkoski, alleged mail robber, was arraigned in Parry Sound police court.

Burowski was wearing a blue suit with a khaki shirt open at the throat, had one finger bandaged and his wrists were bound with handcuffs. He was led into the courtroom by two provincial police officers. He appeared to be a young man, possibly 35 years old. His face, in repose, was gentle. His fair hair looked disarranged. A *Toronto Daily Star* reporter wrote, "During the proceedings he sat quietly, only the searching glances of his eyes, which were downcast and shifty, betrayed his anxiety."

Johnson read the accusation, "John Burowski, you are charged with stealing a Buick coupe on August 18 to the value of $900."

Crown-Attorney W.L. Haight spoke up, "The prisoner is not represented by counsel. I suggest a week's remand without bail." This was granted.

More than a hundred relatives and neighbours gathered Monday afternoon at the small weather-beaten farm house to pay their final respects to the Jackson family. Motor cars lined the roads. Several members of the the McKellar Orange Lodge bore the casket to the hearse and the procession followed along the road to Lakeview Cemetery above the lake at McKellar. A journalist from the Daily Mail and Empire reported, "The Orange burial ritual was used and the casket was lowered into the grave."

The coroner's inquest into the death of Thomas Jackson was held Monday evening in the Parry Sound Courthouse. *The Daily Mail and Empire* reported, "The oak-raftered court room was filled to seating capacity and many stood in the corridor to catch some word of the witnesses."

The first witness called was Dr. Charles S. Applebe who reported on the post-mortem examination of the deceased. He declared that Jackson had sustained a bullet wound to the neck and subsequently died from suffocation induced by blood in the trachea.

The second witness was 20-year-old Haughton Laird. According to Adrian Eric Hayes, "Laird stated that the gunman had fired four shots before Walter tackled him to the ground. He believed that there had also been other shots discharged that morning, but could not say how many or in which direction they had been fired.

"Upon regaining consciousness the prisoner had claimed to be a carpenter working at Bala and told a story of how he had been picked up on the North Road by two men who gave him money and a gun. When the man found out that

HAUGHTON LAIRD

CLAUDE JACKSON

Jackson was dead he offered over $1,800 to Walter and Haughton Laird to release him."

The third witness was Claude Jackson. He was nervous and definitely showed the strain he was suffering after the sad ordeal of burying his father that afternoon. He had to be prompted a number of times by the crown. Claude recalled how a stranger had knocked at their door just before 4 a.m. He pointed to the prisoner and stated, "That man right there."

Claude recalled the stranger said he was from the United States and had accidentally driven his car into a ditch.

Claude told the crown "The prisoner had $1,800 in his pocket and had offered it to me to let him go when he learned that he had shot my father."

He also recalled hearing one of the Laird brothers telling Burowski, "Now, you'll hang. You've shot Mr. Jackson."

Claude heard the prisoner say, "Me shot him? I wish I had shot myself instead."

According to Claude, when Burowski realized that Thomas Jackson was dead he turned to him and said, "Here take this $1,800 out of my pocket. That'll help bury him."

Harold Rolland's testimony at the coroner's inquest revealed that when the first shots were fired he ducked and didn't see much more. He believed that several shots were being fired from the bush.

Adrian Eric Hayes adds, "Inspector E.C. Gurnett of the OPP Criminal Investigation Division in Toronto testified that Thomas

Jackson had been shot by a fragment of a .45 calibre bullet which had ostensibly struck the sharp edge of the steel frame of the Studebaker's rear window and ricochetted. He also added that when apprehended Burowski had been armed with a .45 calibre Colt automatic pistol, from which five shots had been fired."

Coroner M.H. Limbert, M.D. then gave his verdict, "That Jackson came to his death from a bullet wound, fired from a pistol in the hands of John Burowski."

The prisoner sat unshackled between provincial officers and

District Court House, Parry Sound Ontario, where the case was heard.

maintained an unemotional stance when the Coroner read the verdict. Burowski was returned to his jail cell.

A preliminary hearing took place on Friday, August 24 in the Parry Sound courthouse before Police Magistrate James D. Broughton. The hearing was to determine if there was sufficient evidence to commit John Burowski to stand trial for train robbery and for the murder of Thomas Jackson. Attorney Walter Lockwood Haight, KC. represented the province, while John Roland Hett of the Parry Sound legal firm of Weeks and Hett sat counsel for the defense.

The hearing was moved from the Police Court to a much larger room where the Supreme Court sessions occurred in the Parry Sound Courthouse. Newspaper reporters sat elbow to elbow. One reporter described the scene, "Every class and condition of society was represented in the non-descript gathering from gum-chewing flappers in short skirts to careworn mothers with crying babies in their arms."

The same witnesses who shared their testimony at the coroner's inquest were once again asked to tell their stories. However, one additional witness, Walter Laird, who had just been released from hospital, appeared on the stand and told essentially the same story as his brother.

The three mail clerks from the train testified that John Burowski had indeed been one of the three men who had robbed the train on the morning of August 18.

At the close of the hearing Police Magistrate James D. Broughton declared that there was enough evidence for John Burowski to stand trial at the fall assize of the Supreme Court in Parry Sound on the charges of murder and train robbery. The date set for trial was September 26, 1928 with Justice J. Wright of the Supreme Court of Ontario residing.

On September 6, the *Parry Sound North Star* newspaper informed its readers that Burowski had been removed from the Parry Sound Jail. The article stated, "John Burowski mail car bandit has been removed by the authorities to Toronto. This is stated to be for greater safety, as it is feared that attempts may be made at escape. The prisoner will be brought to Parry Sound for trial."

A Toronto reporter described Burowski as sullen and dangerous.

According to the authorities Burowski had written some letters in Polish to some friends in Winnipeg. The letters were intercepted - he wanted his friends to help him break out of prison.

According to Mr. Hayes, "Arrangements were made for his immediate removal by train to Toronto's Don Jail. Here he was placed under the supervision of Major G. Hedley Basher, the governor of the much larger and more secure jail."

Meanwhile, Burowski kept writing letters, this time to a woman in Toronto. He asked her to get confederates to smuggle saws and jimmies into the jail either in food or in clothing. Jail officials ordered a double guard to stand watch over his cell day and night. When no responses came to his letters Burowski grew disturbed. He knew the deck was stacked against him. He had to escape. His last letter implored his friends to aim themselves and rescue him during his journey from Toronto back to Parry Sound, where he was to stand trial. The authorities might transport him by car instead of train and he advised his friends to have a contingency plan for such an emergency.

Burowski on courthose steps during the trial.

Crown Attorney for the District of Parry Sound, Walter Lockwood Haight, KC, had less than four weeks to prepare for the province's case against Burowski. Mr. Hayes adds, "The correspondence that went back and forth during this period between Haight, Inspector John Miller, and Deputy Attorney-General E. Bayly, DC, reveal both uncertainty about Burowski's involvement in the mail car robbery and yet complete confidence that he was guilty of the murder of Thomas Jackson."

On September 13, Inspector Miller wrote to Bayly to advise him that the evidence submitted at Burowski's trial should only be in connection with the theft of the motor car and events leading to the prisoner's arrest, to leave out all reference to the mail robbery. Miller felt that there was evidence which could be submitted by the defense lawyer to throw discredit on several of the Crown's witnesses, namely the three mail-car clerks. He completed the letter by writing: "While the Crown witnesses may be correct in their belief that the prisoner Burowski was one of the men in the mail-car holdup, there are certain facts which cast a feeling of doubt."

On the basis of Miller's advice, Bayly wrote to Haight on the following day: "It occurred to me that in the murder charge there is no necessity to go into the mail-car robbery with any detail. If we succeed in arresting the two other men charged, there is no object in being embarrassed with evidence on the robbery charge...and which would in no way add to the chance of proof against Burowski on the murder charge."

This opinion quickly changed when officials received Burowski's criminal record from the United States. The documents revealed that Burowski, alias Stanley Zinwz, alias John Bryda, had once been incarcerated at the Pennsylvania State Prison and also at Rockland, and Auburn, New York for armed robbery and discharging a firearm with intent to kill. It would seem Burowski was capable of murder.

John Roland Hett, legal counsel for the defendant tried in vain to postpone the trial or change vicinity. When he appealed to the Attorney-General of Ontario this was his response. "My own view would be that men of this kind are very dangerous for this Province. He was responsible for the death of one of our citizens. He was engaged in an indictable offense at the time he was apprehended. His record, as we have received it, is bad. I cannot see how the postponing of the trial would benefit his case. A speedy trial for these offenders is the best way to rid the country of undesirable citizens."

It seems the Attorney-General had already convicted his client.

Adrian Eric Hayes in his article 'Lawyer's Change of Venue Refused' records what happened next, "On the morning of September 24, 1928 a handcuffed John Burowski was taken from the Don Jail into a waiting car escorted by Inspectors John Miller and William Stringer, and guarded by several heavily armed constables.

Once in the police car, leg-irons were placed on his ankles. At Union Station a special coach, coupled directly to the locomotive, was waiting for him. The coach was isolated from the rest of the train by the baggage car. Ironically, in a Pullman coach to the rear of the train were Alexander M. Gibson, District Superintendent of Railway Mail Services, and the three mail clerks who had been subpoenaed to testify about the mail car holdup."

The trial of John Burowski began on the morning of September 25. John Hett tried again to postpone the trial so he could adequately prepare. He also claimed Burowski had an alibi for the time of the robbery.

The Crown Attorney Walter L. Haight responded by stating that no argument was worth considering for an adjournment. He main-

Form II—(Section 671)

SUMMONS TO WITNESS

CANADA
PROVINCE OF ONTARIO
DISTRICT OF PARRY SOUND.

To *Walter Laird*
of the *Town* of *Parry Sound* in the district of
Parry Sound, *Expressman*
(Occupation)

WHEREAS information has been laid before the undersigned

J. D. Broughton, a justice of the peace in and for the said

District of Parry Sound, that **at the Township of Ferguson, on the**

As in the summons or warrant against the accused

Eighteenth day of August, 1928, John Burkowsky did murder one

Thomas Jackson.

and it has been made to appear to me that you are likely to give material evidence

for **Prosecution,** . These are therefore to require you to be and to
(The prosecution or the accused)

appear before me on **Friday** next at **10.30** o'clock in the

Fore noon at **The Court House, Parry Sound, Ontario,**

or before such other justice or justices of the peace of the said district of Parry
Sound as shall then be there, to testify what you know concerning the said charge

so made against the said **John Burkowsky,** as aforesaid.

HEREIN FAIL NOT.

GIVEN under my hand and seal this **Twenty-third,** day of **August**

in the year of our Lord 19**28** at **Parry Sound,** in the District aforesaid.

J D Broughton

J. P., district of Parry Sound.

tained that the issue at hand was whether Burowski was guilty of the murder of Thomas Jackson. His involvment in the train robbery was secondary.

The Honourable Justice W.H. Wright of the High Court Division of the Supreme Court of Ontario listened intently and finally responded that there was insufficient grounds for a postponement of the trial or change of venue.

Burowski was then led into the courtroom by police officials and placed in the dock where he entered a plea of not guilty to the charge of murder. At this point Hett stood his ground and requested a need for more time to secure his witnesses. Justice Wright acknowledged the request and stayed the trial until 9:30 the next morning. The Crown stated to Hett that subpoenas would be issued right away for the witnesses whose testimony he required.

Ironically, an Order-in-Council approved by the Lieutenant-Governor of Ontario the day before authorized rewards of $500, $350, and $200 to be paid to Walter, Haughton and Harold for the capture of Burowski. According to Adrian Hayes, "As early as August 25 Crown Attorney Walter Lockwood Haight had written to the Deputy Attorney-General suggesting that province also pay rewards of $100 to Walter, and $500 each to Haughton and Harold."

Another letter written on August 30 addressed to the Attorney-General, by the Commissioner of the Ontario Provincial Police, Major General V.A.S. William stated, "I consider this is a case where the Government of this Province might be generous as it was entirely due to the bravery and initiative of the Laird brothers, assisted by Rolland, that the murderer of Jackson was apprehended, as the robbery and pursuit of the robbers occurred before the police were notified."

It seems that Mr. Burowski was convicted before his trial was over.

At 9:30 a.m. on September 26 the trial resumed and continued until 8 p.m.

Hett claimed that the shots fired from the bushes after his client had been subdued could have killed Jackson. On cross-examination he was able to get the Laird brothers to admit that no one actually had seen Burowski shoot Jackson. Hett also pointed out that if one of Burowski's bullets had indeed hit Jackson, he had not been the intended victim. Burowski was shooting in self-defense because he believed the Laird brothers to be armed.

However, Hett encountered some trouble when Claude Jackson, the son of the murder victim, took the stand. Claude described how his father was standing at the rear of the Studebaker holding a lantern when the shooting started. He added that the type of lantern his father held would extinguish when dropped (in order to prevent forest fires). At the time Burowski began shooting Claude looked to see the place where his father was standing and saw the lantern was out. Yet, Claude was unable to state that he had actually seen Burowski shoot his dad.

According to a story that appeared in *True Canadian Detective Stories*, "Walter Laird swore he had seen the Colt .45 taken from Burowski and that no one else had been firing or had firearms as far as he knew. As Laird said 'I saw the prisoner fire three shots,' Burowski who had been listening closely to the evidence, opened his mouth wide and sat in an attitude of amazement which he held until after Laird had sworn that he personally had been wounded."

The North Star newspaper reported, "The evidence of the Crown witness was practically the same as that published by the preliminary trial following the shooting. Burowski was placed in the witness box and admitted that he had been committed to the penitentiary in Pennsylvania, also at Rockland, and Auburn New York for shooting with intent to kill and for robbery."

The True Canadian Detective article added, "When Crown Counsel Haight tried to draw Burowski out concerning his past life of crime in the United States, he angrily stated that the police had questioned him so insistently that he was 'nearly driven silly'."

His account of the shooting read, "I was sitting in the car and a boy comes up and asks me if I need help. I said I had help. Then one of the men pointed something at me and says, 'Hands up! You are in a stolen car!' So I say, 'What's the matter with you, eh?' and he says again, 'You are in a stolen car, get out of here!' So I get out with my hands up.

"I see one fellow coming at me from the front of the car. Then someone starts shooting and a bullet gets me in the finger. So then I get excited and start to shoot.

I could easily have broken loose from these fellows but I didn't want to hurt these little boys."

The trial was nearing a close. The jury was out and everyone waited in anticipation of the verdict. After 75 minutes of deliberation the jury returned.

It was 4:30 p.m. on September 27, 1928, when John Burowski returned to the courtroom for sentencing. The Honourable Justice W.H. Wright spoke, "I do not wish to add to your remorse in this, which must be the most terrible hour of your life. You have had a fair trial. You have been well defended. Murder is one of the most serious crimes known to British and Canadian Law. It is a crime not only against man, but against God. Everyone who takes a human life, who sweeps a fellow being into eternity, must pay the penalty. The jury has found you guilty of the murder of Thomas Jackson, and I have no alternative."

One reporter later wrote that Burowski clenched his jaws and a tear rolled down his cheek on hearing the verdict.

When the Judge asked him if he had anything to say he stated, "I believe I have got no justice. I'm not guilty of this charge."

He was then sentenced to be hanged at Parry Sound jail on Friday, December 7, 1928 at 12:30 a.m.

It would seem the Burowski story had come to a close. The Town of Parry Sound began preparations to honour their heroes who had apprehended a dangerous criminal without the benefit of firearms. On November 20, Parry Sound council awarded cheques and letters of appreciation to the Laird brothers and Harold Rolland. Mayor Johnson even presented engraved wrist watches to the brothers and a mantel clock to Rolland. Letters of appreciation were written such as this one, "One of the outstanding attributes of the British people has always been that they respected the law. Canadians are following faithfully in these footsteps. If our citizens fail to uphold the arm of the law then anarchy must ensue. No country can survive anarchy. When every man is

𝕷𝖔𝖞𝖆𝖑 𝕺𝖗𝖆𝖓𝖌𝖊 𝖄𝖔𝖚𝖓𝖌 𝕭𝖗𝖎𝖙𝖔𝖓 𝕬𝖘𝖘𝖔𝖈𝖎𝖆𝖙𝖎𝖔𝖓

COUNTY LODGE FOR NIPISSING AND PARRY SOUND

30 Regina street,
North Bay, February 11, 1929.

W. Laird, Esq.,
Parry Sound, Ont.

Dear Sir and Brother:-

                I was instructed by motion made in
Annual session of County lodge for the District of Nipissing
and Parry Sound, held at North Bay, Saturday February 9th 1929,
to write you a letter, expressing their appreciation and comm-
endation for your actions, which were to a large extent, responsible for bringing to justice, a certain criminal during the
month of July 1928.

                        Yours fraternally,

                        Geo E Thompson

                        County Secretary.

Letter

a law unto himself the established institutions of our country must fail..."

No one had any idea that John Hett was still attempting to obtain a new trial for Burkowski. It was learned on December 5, that Thomas Mulvey, Under Secretary of State, had telegraphed the Attorney-General to tell him that the Governor-General would not intercede in the sentence of the Supreme Court. Construction workers were busy erecting a scaffold in the jail courtyard. Excitement in the town was high as the time drew closer to the hanging. John Burowski had just been transported from Toronto to Parry Sound to await his appointment with death.

On the same day John Burowski swore out an affidavit before Sheriff James E.T. Armstrong admitting his involvement in the holdup and implicating two other men. According to his statement, it had been his job to locate and steal a car in Parry Sound for the get-away after the arrival of the train. Adrian Hayes, from his own research of the case, points out "Under the stipulations of the Ontario Freedom of Information and Privacy Act, the names of the two men implicated by Burowski as the train bandits have been censored from the affidavit with a black magic marker."

We do know that the first man was Canadian and the second an American.

It was further learned by Hett that several bullets had been removed by police officials from the gate where Thomas Jackson had been found lying on the ground. Hett knew that these shots could not have come from Burowski's gun.

Adrian Hayes adds, "Just after 5 o'clock in the afternoon of December 5, John Hett delivered an application for a temporary stay of execution to Osgoode Hall with an affidavit offering new evidence in the case for which Burowski had been convicted. That evening several other judges of the Supreme Court of Ontario went to the home of Justice John Millar McEvoy to discuss the case." Time was running out.

The Evening Telegram reported, "Burowski was given the last rites of the Church by Father Gregory Kelly early yesterday evening, after eating sparsely of a meal of pork, potatoes and pumpkin pie.

The scaffold had been tried by Hangman Ellis early in the afternoon. Burowski sat in his cell from 6 until midnight, a mental wreck. About every three minutes he demanded from his guard to know whether further word had not been received from his counsel. From 10 until five minutes to 12 o'clock he sat swaying his head from side to side in the death cell."

At approximately 18 minutes prior to his hanging word arrived that the condemned man had been granted a two week reprieve. The Telegram added, "Then came the word of respite. His enthusiasm and evident relief knew no bounds. Borowski said, 'I will probably get 20 years now.'

"By reason of the narrow confines of the jail and jailyard at Parry Sound, John Burowski, who was to have been executed this morning, has had the harrowing experience during the past few days of not only hearing, but seeing the workmen erecting the scaffold upon which he was to die."

It was soon learned, however, that police officials were unable to track down and apprehend the two suspects cited in Burowski's affidavit. On December 15, John Hett received a call from Attorney-General Bayly to inform him that the investigation into the Burowski case had been closed. This prompted Hett to write another letter to the Attorney-General stating, "Had Burowski been given the opportunity to normally confer with Counsel previous to his being put on trial, the above facts and probably many others would almost certainly have been dealt with at the trial...

"I cannot help feeling that the attitude of your Department has been the attitude of the ordinary citizen who says or thinks in substance, 'a man has been killed, there was a foreigner mixed up in the affair; the foreigner has a bad record and no great injustice will be done if he is hanged although it will be necessary, before taking that step, to give him a trial...'"

It was over for John Burowski.

The snow was falling that fateful night of December 21. The wind was howling and blowing to chill the warmest clothed spectator. A small group gathered beneath the gallows and waited to witness the hanging. *The Toronto Star* reported that hangman

Arthur Ellis appeared jumpy and snapped at a young reporter who touched the rope prior to the hanging. Ellis shouted, "Leave that alone!". He also ordered those standing on the platform to get off. The time was nearing 1:15 a.m.

Adrian Hayes describes what happened next, "After Burowski appeared it was just a short eight seconds from the time he ascended the stairs of the gallows until the time he fell through the trap door to his death. The jail surgeon subsequently pronounced that death had been instantaneous."

Just after the hanging Ellis turned to a reporter of the *Toronto Star* and stated, "There was no hitch anywhere. I am glad of it. My only fear is that sometime I may make a mistake and inflict unnecessary torture on the prisoner."

The Globe wrote, "John Burowski paid with his life early this (Friday) morning for the murder of Thomas Jackson. Burowski went to the scaffold at Parry Sound Jail at 1:15 a.m. and was pronounced dead 15 minutes later.

Sheriff J.E. Armstrong told *The Globe* that the man "retained his composure to the last."

John Burowski was buried in the jailhouse courtyard face-downward. As suspicion had it, this would prevent him from going to heaven.

Young Blanche Grant had followed the story closely since the robbery. As a curious young girl she couldn't help but visit the jail. Her impression remains in print. She wrote, "When the jail authority built the scaffold I saw the top beam of it looking over the high walls of the jail's courtyard. Though the robber committed this capital crime, people in town did not want to see the man hung here which I could not understand. Because of the public outcry, the wall height was increased by a solid paper fence on the day of the execution. My father told me that at midnight of that crucial day the courtyard was ablaze with lights and the shadows of the action could be seen on the paper fence. Yet what he never told me, but what I heard years later, was that at this last public hanging in Parry Sound many people sat on the roofs of the surrounding houses and witnessed the hanging."

Parry Sound had indeed had its four months of not only mystery and intrique but also the notoriety of a trial and a gruesome hanging. Unfortunately, it is probable that the wrong man was hung. John Burowski paid the ultimate price for one of his partners - whose identity, ironically, is protected by law.

- From 1867 to 1962 Canada executed 704 people.

- Canada executed 11 women during the death penalty years. Margaret Pitre of Quebec was the last in 1949.

- In January 1968 Parliament passed a law that only those who murdered a police officer, a prison guard or killed someone during the commission of another crime were eligible to be hanged.

- Parliament voted to abolish capital punishment in 1976 by a six-vote margin.

- At the time of abolishment 11 people were on death row.

- Thirty-eight U.S. states have death penalty laws on the books.

Bibliography

Boyer, Robert J., *A Good Town Grew Here*, Herald-Gazette Press, Bracebridge, 1975

Fleming Grant, Blanche E., *The Great Parry Sound Train Robbery Caper*, Morsel Press, Nobel, 1987

Craick, W. Arnot, P*ort Hope Historical Sketches*, The Williamson Press, Port Hope, 1901

Guillet, Edwin, *Cobourg 1798-1948*, Goodfellow Printing Company Limited, Oshawa, 1948

Miller, Orlo, *London 200*. London Chamber of Commerce, 1992.

Miller, Orlo, *This Was London*. Butternut Press Inc. Westport, Ontario, 1998

Symons, Doug M., *The Village that Straddled a Swamp*. The Oxford Historical Society, 1997.

Newspapers

The London Home Bank Robbery:

The London Evening Free Press, London, February 9, 1924

The London Morning Advertiser, London, February 5, April 11, 12, 1924

The London Free Press, London, February 7, April 10, 1924

The London Evening Free Press, London, September 3, 5, 6, 12, 1921

The London Advertiser, London, September 6, 1921

Bronson, L.N., *The London Free Press*, London, December 4, 1974

The London Free Press, London, November 21, 1987

The London Free Press, London, November 16, 1991

Neely, Alastair, Wells, Barry, *The London Free Press*, London, May 15, 1997

The Great Parry Sound Train Robbery:

The Daily Mail and Empire, Toronto, August 20, 21, 1928

The Toronto Daily Star, Toronto, August 20, 1928

The Evening Telegram, Toronto, August 20, December 7, 17, 1928

The North Star, Parry Sound, September 6, 27, November 22, 1928

The Globe and Mail, Toronto, December 7, 1928

Hayes, Adrian Eric, *The Parry Sound North Star*, Parry
      Sound, August 25, September 1, 7, 21, 1989.

Evil Visits the Goderich Fall Fair:

The Signal, Goderich, September 29, October 20, 27, 1910,
      April 13, 20, June 15, 1911

The Love-Sick Doctor:

Stevenson, Kevin, *The Cobourg Sentinel Star*, Cobourg, June 14,
      16, 19, 22, 23, 1978

Ballad of a Murderer:

The Daily Sentinel Review, Woodstock, September 19, 1890

The Globe, Woodstock, September 22, 23, 24, 25, 26, 27, 29, 30,
      October 1, 3, 1890

The Toronto Star Weekly, Toronto, September 26, 1925

The London Free Press, London, October 29, 1990

Woodstock's Deadly Tea Leaves:

The Daily Sentinel Review, Woodstock, September 23, 25, 28, 30,
      October 2, December 17, 1935

An Alternative to Divorce in Port Hope:

The Port Hope Weekly Guide, Port Hope, October 6, 13, 27, 1893,
      January 3, 12, 19, 26, June 8, 22, 1894

Other Periodicals:

Duarte, Joe, Dying to run away from home, *This Week*, Oshawa, Sunday, April 2, 2000

Duarte, Joe, The Fires of Desire, *This Week*, Oshawa, Sunday March 5, 2000

Winter, Brian, The trial of Archie McLaughlin, *Whitby Free Press*, August, 1980.

Stewart, Irene, *The Ribbon*, Early Canadian Life Magazine, Toronto, June 1980

The Kingston Gazette, Kingston, June 8, 13, October 7, 1840, July 2, November 5, 1842, March 5, August 19, 1843

Local Man Charged With Murder of Hon. Thomas D'Arcy McGee, *Ottawa Citizen*, Ottawa, Friday April 17, 1868

New Liskeard Speaker, New Liskeard, Thursday, July 25, 1929

Pays With Life on Scaffold for Killing Woman, *The Haileyburian*, Haileybury, June 16, 1932

Chinaman Hanged at Haileybury Jail Yard, *New Liskeard Speaker*, New Liskeard Speaker, Thursday, January 14, 1937

Murderer Hanged at Haileybury, *Temiskaming Speaker*, Temiskaming, Thursday, June 16, 1949

Brethour Girl's Body Found Murderedr - Confesses Crime, *Temiskaming Speaker*, Temiskaming, June 15, 1961

Currie, Ted, The Story of Bracebridge's Hanging, *The Muskoka Sun*, Thursday, September 10, 1998

Crime in Pioneer Muskoka, *The Muskokan*, Thursday, August 6, 1987

The Last Hanging in Muskoka, *The Muskoka Sun*, Thursday, July 5, 1979

Photo Credits

Index

Notes

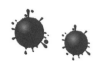